JUICING FOR WEIGHT LOSS

200 Delicious Juicing Recipes That Help You Lose Weight Naturally Fast, Gain energy, and Detox| with 3-Week Weight Loss Juicing Meal Plan

MYRA J. BATTY

Table of Contents

Foreword

Why would anyone want to drink fruits and vegetables instead of eating them? Well, our bodies need nutrients, and these nutrients are better taken in an easily digestible form, such as in juice. During the digestion process, whole foods are broken down by chewing first before the nutrients can be absorbed by the body. Juicing takes the same function as chewing; it breaks down the cell wall of the plants and makes the nutrients available for absorption. Basically, juicing eliminates the need for chewing and makes the nutrients readily available for absorption immediately the juice is ingested. The body can then put those nutrients to work in as little as 15 to 20 minutes. Some say they can feel their green juice kicking in as soon as they drink it. Even though juices are highly nutritious, they should not completely replace whole foods. You would however have to eat a lot of vegetables to load up on the amount of nutrition that's available in just one glass of juice.

As you get started on this book, I hope you are pairing juicing with healthy diet, and if you aren't, you should consider it. And don't forget to stay active while you're at it. Weight loss is best when you adjust your whole lifestyle, that way the results are more permanent and there is minimal chance of falling back into unhealthy habits.

Juicing is healthy but it is not a magic bullet that will burn fat while you do nothing. There's not a miracle that comes with juicing only but there are numerous benefits for your general health, brain health, heart health, immune system, mental health, blood vessel and bone health. Juicing also helps in detoxification. Juicing is a seemingly a straightforward thing. Pick your preferred ingredients and make your juice using a juicer, right? Well, not exactly. When it comes to juicing for weight loss, there are a few things that you will need to pay attention to, such as the source of the fresh products you choose, how you prepare for juicing, how to properly store the juice as well as ensuring to juice a variety of vegetables and rotating them.

This book will help you get familiar with juicing for weight loss as well as provide you with recipes that are sure to help you lose those inches that you intend to. Juicing is particularly helpful to the people who may find it hard to eat their fruits and vegetables.

Introduction

I am personally in love with the most popular diet today-Keto diet- as it has changed my life completely. People like me would like to follow Keto life style but, some of you are confused of where to start and how to plan your Keto meals. In this edition, you will get to know the simplest Keto eating plans and viable Keto diet tips for your wonderful Keto journey. While you follow Keto life style, you will be focused more on healthy fats, with proteins and moderately less carbohydrates. You will get the nutrients mainly from vegetables. While you are in Keto diet, your body burns fat for energy rather than carbs or sugar, which is named as 'Ketosis'. Thus you can burn your body fat through Ketosis and will contribute to weight loss. The benefits of Keto diet are endless as you will feel more mental clarity as well as more energy levels and reduced inflammation. It is also helpful for conditions like obesity, epilepsy, neurological conditions, and ultimately to enhance your endurance.

The lesson I learned while following the diet was initially, I used to feel like eating more for satisfying my hunger. But after a few days my body adapted to the diet and I didn't feel hungry at even meal time. So if you don't feel hungry, there is no need to eat your food. But ensure the water intake is sufficient for your body. This book is mainly intended to people who sincerely wish to follow Keto diet and want realistic results. It extensively covers the topics like Basics of the Ketogenic Diet, foods to include and avoid in Keto diet, as well as important tips for successful Keto diet. The recipe session exclusively covers delicious yet simple and easy Keto meals which you can prepare using 5 or less ingredients. So move forward and explore Keto journey. It's a pleasure to welcome you to the amazing life of ketosis.

Chapter 1
Basic of Juicing

Juicing explained

To put is plainly, juicing refers to the process of extracting juice from fruits and vegetables. The juice contains most of the vitamins, minerals, and plant chemicals (phytonutrients) found in the whole fruit or vegetable. As a health trend, 'juicing' is the practice of increasing daily intake of fresh fruits and vegetables by drinking fresh juices. There are numerous reasons for people to adopt juicing, most are usually health related. Juicing does more than increase your intake of healthy nutrients, it could help you to reset your system so that you crave healthy foods, it provides benefits for weight loss, it boosts your immune system, it helps in detoxification, it eases digestion and reduces inflammation, and it promotes beautiful clear skin among many other benefits. Juicing has become a popular way for people to ease symptoms of health conditions that can be improved through diet. There are people suffering from depression, fibromyalgia, irritable bowel syndrome, and even eczema who have seen a great improvement after they started juicing. In the world of nutrition and dietetics, there is a division on whether juicing is healthier than eating fruit and vegetables. While it is true that a significant portion of the fiber content of fruits and vegetables is lost during the juicing process, it is important to note that the fruits and vegetables most popular for juicing have a high water content and are therefore not the best sources of insoluble fiber anyway. In order to counter the loss of insoluble fiber, you should strive to eat meals that include high fiber foods such as whole grains, beans as well as raw or cooked vegetables to ensure you get the insoluble fiber necessary for digestion.

Juicing for weight loss

When you settle on juicing as something that you would like to incorporate into your lifestyle in the long-term, you can invest in a juicer and make it a habit to always have fresh produce stocked up in your refrigerator or pantry so that you always have the necessary ingredients on hand.

For a healthy and long-lasting weight loss, the transition to juicing is vital. It is something that you should take you time to do because if you make the changes too drastic or sudden, you may cause stress on your digestive system and that may come with many unpleasant side effects. For starters, you can try to replace one of your meals with a glass of fresh juice. It will work different for everyone but a good place to start is by taking juice as the first meal of the day, on an empty stomach. In the case that your regular If your typical diet consists mainly of processed foods, a sudden increase in fiber content could spell trouble for your digestive system. The best way to go about it would be to replace a single meal at a time with juice to help ease your body into the transition.

Along with juicing, you may want to consider intermittent fasting which is among the less strict diets which can very easily become a lifestyle. While most diets dictate what you should or shouldn't eat, intermittent fasting only focuses on the scheduling of your meals. While there are many ways to do it, one way may involve restricting your meals to a 6- or 8-hour window during the day or choosing specific days of the week during which you restrict yourself to just one meal a day.

Intermittent fasting encourages the body to get energy from burning fat that is already stored in the body after using up the energy available from food. As with any other diet, you should always consult your doctor or dietician before getting stated. Intermittent fasting and juicing go well together because taking healthy beverages and staying hydrated is necessary, and juices make a perfect snack for the hours that you're not eating. Juicing makes it possible to load up on the necessary vitamins and minerals. Another thing with juices is that they offer a very healthy way to break a fast, especially considering that the best time to take juice is on an empty stomach, that way the body makes the most of it. Intermittent fasting is a good option for anyone looking for a long-term diet. If you choose to make it a daily routine, the first thing is to determine the number of hours a day during which you will schedule your meals. This should of course be determined by your daily schedule. While the focus with intermittent fasting is not what you eat but when you eat, if you're trying to stay healthy, be sure to watch what you eat as well. It is okay to snack on healthy beverages such as natural juices while practicing intermittent fasting

Handling fresh produce

Some things to pay attention to when choosing fresh produce to purchase is how they have been grown, certified organic are best. The age of your produce and how it has been stored will influence how good and healthy it is.

When to Buy: For maximum flavor and nutrition and also to help with budgeting, maximize locally grown or seasonal produce. If you can, grow your own greens that you can harvest and juice immediately. Only buy fruits and vegetables that will be in good condition by the time you are turning on your juicer. Fresher produce is always better for juicing

How to Wash: Properly wash your produce to remove dirt and bacteria and reduce pesticide residues. Washing under running water and rubbing with your hand or a vegetable brush. The water temperature should close to that of the produce you are washing. An alternative is to use a vinegar-water solution with 1 part vinegar to 3 parts water. You can soak hard produce in a sink filled with cold water and 4 tablespoons of baking soda for 5 to 15 minutes then rinse them under running water, giving them a scrub. Leafy greens can be soaked for a short time, 2 minutes then rinsed under running water. Delicate berries can be rinsed quickly with the baking soda water, rinsed again under clean running water.

Prepping your produce: Trim the ends of root vegetables (such as carrots and beets), as these areas can harbor bacteria. Remove the very outer colored part of oranges, grapefruits, and mandarins as the volatile oils in these rinds are difficult to digest. Retain as much of the white pith as you can because this area contains valuable nutrients. The rinds of lemons and limes can be removed or left on depending on your preference. Red beets can be peeled to reduce their earthy flavor and any limp leaves and any damaged areas or bad spots on your produce should be removed.

What to Do with Pulp: Juice pulp can be added to baked goods and soups or dehydrated into crackers and if you are capable of. Compost the pulp or find a neighbor or farm that can compost it or use it in some way.

Storing your juice: it is best to consume your juice when it is fresh, but if you must store it remember:

- Oxygen will make the juice go bad faster so use canning jars with a lid and a screw band lid you can and make sure to fill the jar to the rim or use a vacuum sealer to remove the air.
- Store your juice in the coldest part of your refrigerator. You can also place your filled juice jars in the freezer for 10 to 15 minutes to speed the cooling process before transferring them to the refrigerator, set a timer if you are likely to forget.
- Adding some lemon or lime to the juice will help maintain the freshness for longer.

SOME ADVANTAGES OF JUICING INCLUDE:
- Juice is tasty and you can disguise the flavor of your less liked vegetables by combining them with your favorite fruits.
- You can get your juice quickly and easily and carry it as an on-the-go meal or snack.
- In case you would likesome more fiber content, simply add some of the pulp to it.
- You have the freedom to choose your preferred ingredients and adjust to your own taste.
- Juicing is a great way to get younger children to get the nutrient from fruits and vegetables.
- Pulp that is leftover from juicing can be used in baked goods, such as muffins and breads, or as a base for homemade stocks and broths.

Tips for juicing
- If you are counting calories, remember that it is more difficult to measure the calories in liquids than in solid foods, so be careful with your intake of juices.
- If you decide to start on a juice cleanse or fat, do not overextend it as this will slow down your metabolism and eventually make it hard to lose weight in the future.
- Prioritize a smooth transition to juicing as this will make it easier to stick to.
- Losing weight too quickly on a juicing regimen is unhealthy, and the weight loss you achieve is unlikely to last.
- Always wash your produce before juicing. Consider going completely organic if you can. Commercial may be laced with pesticides and fertilizers that can be damaging to your health.
- Consume juice within a day or two to avoid it going bad. Remember homemade juice has no preservatives and therefore has a very short shelf life.
- Avoid fasting if you are engaging in a juicing regimen because you may suffer negative side effects such as headaches, dizziness, fatigue, and irritability.
- Consult your doctor before embarking on a juicing journey. While it is a healthy option, it may not work positively for everyone.

This meal plan is for those who are bold enough to take on a big challenge and make big changes to get big results. It will not be easy, but it will be well worth the effort. Before you start, ensure to get a green light from your doctor and make the necessary lifestyle adjustments for best results. The importance of getting support from a doctor or dietician while undertaking a juicing diet for weight loss cannot be overemphasized. There are no hard fast rules for the juicing diet, and you are free to make adjustment to suit your personal preferences. This diet is not suitable for long-term use so do not consider it for long period of dieting. It is, however, best for short-term weight loss sprints. While progressing through the diet, if you experience any physical discomfort, such as feeling fatigue or lethargic, you need to stop and adjust the plan.

Week 1

An important point to note is that you must ease your body into the juicing diet, any sudden drastic changes may cause problems and probably negate the whole point of juicing, so take your time to safely get started. To do this, you can start with 5 days of juicing as well as eating, as you slowly get rid of processed foods, fast food and foods that are high in saturated fats. You should focus on getting your nutrients from plant-based foods. You can also gradually reduce your portions while paying attention to how your body responds. Doing this under the guidance of a dietician will ensure a safe and healthy weight loss. While following this meal plan, it is vital that you hydrate as often as possible. Everyone's fluid requirements differ so listen to your body and respond accordingly.

It is normal to experience some withdrawal symptoms for the first few days of juicing as your body adapts to juicing. Give yourself some time and be very keen with the cues your body is giving. If you try one week of juicing and would like to challenge yourself then go ahead and take on the second week.

	DAY 1	DAY 2	DAY 3	DAY 4	DAY5	DAY 6	DAY 7
Wake up	5 Minute Berry Loaded Refreshing Juice (119.9)	5 Minute Fruity Juice with Spinach (85.9)	Lemony Carrots and Pepper Lettuce Juice (88.9)	Zucchini Plus Broccoli and Kale Juice (52.9)	Gingery Fennel Spinach and Celery Juice (97.9)	Kale Grapefruit and Cucumber Juice (64.9)	5 Minute Tangy Kale Celery Juice (22.9)
Breakfast	Limey Orange and Kiwi Juice (103)	Apple Chia and Spinach with Mint (73.9)	Mango Kale and Spinach Celery Juice (85.9)	Tangy Romaine Lettuce and Beet (62.9)	10 Minute Clementine and Celery Juice (95.9)	Beet Cabbage Green Juice with Pineapple (56.9)	Celery Chard and Basil Refreshing Juice (117.9)
Lunch	5 Minute Berry Loaded Refreshing Juice (119.9)	Watermelon Zucchini and Limey Coconut Water (81.9)	Kale Celery Berry Juice with Cucumber (83.9)	Kale Cabbage and Plum Cocktail (79.9)	Apple Berry Green Tea Juice with Spinach (65.9)	Carrot Apple and Celery Energizing Juice (76.9)	Collard Leaves and Blackberry Power Juice (29.9)

Afternoon snack	10 Minute Healthy Ulcer Care Drink (87.9)	5 Minute Fruity Juice with Spinach (85.9)	Peppered Broccoli Cucumber and Green Leaves (80.9)	Tangy Chad with Beet Cucumber Juice (75.9)	Yellow Peppers Blended with Limey Spinach (44.9)	Kale Grapefruit and Cucumber Juice (64.9)	5 Minute Lettuce Sprouts Celery Juice (54.9)
Dinner	Grapefruits Plus Peas and Carrots Juice (89.9)	Watermelon Zucchini and Limey Coconut Water (81.9)	Mango Kale and Spinach Celery Juice (85.9)	Gingered Apple Cucumber Detox Juice (83.9)	10 Minute Clementine and Celery Juice (95.9)	5 Minute Spinach Berry and Coconut Juice (72.9)	Gingery Cucumber and Kale Cilantro Juice (102)
Dessert	10 Minute Healthy Ulcer Care Drink (87.9)	Plum Tomato Cucumber and Peppered Gazpacho (111)	Gingery Fennel Spinach and Celery Juice (97.9)	Strawberry and Romaine Juice with Carrots (101)	Yellow Peppers Blended with Limey Spinach (44.9)	5 Minute Cucumber Celery Limey Juice (97.9)	Celery Chard and Basil Refreshing Juice (117.9)
Bedtime	Limey Orange and Kiwi Juice (103)	Aloe Sprout and Cabbage Juice (90.9)	Asparagus Apple and Celery Energizing Juice (60.9)	Kale Cabbage and Plum Cocktail (79.9)	Spinach Carrots and Celery Juice (68.9)	Carrot Apple and Celery Energizing Juice (76.9)	5 Minute Pear and Celery Juice (56.9)
Total calories	711.5	611.4	584.3	536.4	514.3	511.3	502.4

Week 2

Congratulations for coming this far! At this point, it is most likely that your body has gone through the withdrawal and has adapted to juicing. You're also more confident and have a better idea of which juices you like better and which ones make you feel more energetic. Feel free to experiment and adjust the recipes to suit your personal preferences. As usual, remember to hydrate as much as your body needs and if you're having trouble following the plan, you can adjust it to suit you.

	DAY 1	DAY 2	DAY 3	DAY 4	DAY 5	DAY 6	DAY 7
Wake Wake up	Aloe Vera and Cabbage Cleanser (90.9)	Orange and Ginger Root Energy Shot (100)	Minty Chi Spinach and Apple Juice (73.9)	Minute Kale Berry Green Juice (83.9) 83.9	Quick and Simple Green Juice (72.9)	Cacao Powder Kale Raspberry Juice (103.9)	Lettuce and Carrots Salad Juice (88.9)

Breakfast	Easy Banana Berry Cilantro Juice (91.9)	Pineapple Jalapeno and Cilantro Juice (70.9)	5 Minute Pear and Celery Juice (56.9)	Celery Spinach and Carrots Healing Drink (68.9)	Pear Parsley and Orange Juice (50.9)	Orange Potato and Turmeric Roots Refresher (85.9)	5 Minute Honeydew and Asparagus Lemonade (33.9)
Lunch	Pear and Parsley with Orange Juice (99)	Radish and Carrot Garlicky Detox Juice (89.9)	Quite Lime and Grapefruit Juice (86.9)	10 Minute Kale Berry Green Juice (83.9)	Apple Cinnamon Anti-Inflammatory Juice (105)	5 Minute Lemony Cabbage Celery Juice 50.9	Tangy Kale plus Bok Choy Drink (52.9)
Afternoon snack	Easy and Quick Lettuce Celery Juice (72.9)	Quick and Healthy Carrots Cantaloupe Juice (79.9)	Minty Chi Spinach and Apple Juice (73.9)	Swiss Chard with Broccoli and Apple Juice (50.9)	Celery Cucumber and Orange Spinach Cleanser (56.9)	Orange Potato and Turmeric Roots Refresher (85.9)	Lettuce and Carrots Salad Juice (88.9)
Dinner	Aloe Vera and Cabbage Cleanser (90.9)	5 Minute Fruity Weight Loss Juice (83.9)	Ginger Spinach and Grapefruit Juice (70.9)	Celery Spinach and Carrots Healing Drink (68.9)	Pear Parsley and Orange Juice (50.9)	Gingered Kiwi Papaya and Coconut Water (37.9)	Tangy Kale plus Bok Choy Drink (52.9)
Dessert	Easy Banana Berry Cilantro Juice (91.9)	Minty Cucumbers and Gingered Carrot Juice (93.9)	Veggie Boosted Detox Juice with Ginger (70.9)	Cinnamon Berry and Gingered Spinach Juice (94.9)	Quick and Simple Green Juice (72.9)	Beet Cucumber and Cabbage Juice (55.9)	5 Minute Honeydew and Asparagus Lemonade (33.9)
Bedtime	Pear and Parsley with Orange Juice (99)	Quick and Healthy Carrots Cantaloupe Juice (79.9)	Ginger Spinach and Grapefruit Juice (70.9)	Swiss Chard with Broccoli and Apple Juice (50.9)	Celery Cucumber and Orange Spinach Cleanser (56.9)	Gingered Kiwi Papaya and Coconut Water (37.9)	Gingery Grapefruit and Orange Juice (24.9)
Total calories	636.5	598.4	504.3	502.3	466.4	458.3	376.3

Week 3

It is advisable to add protein powders to your juice after day 14 of the diet. Anything unsweetened, unflavored and plant based will do. Take more water or coconut water if you feel dizzy or have headaches or if you are exercising more than you usually do. When juicing exclusively, consider adding olive oil to your juice at dinner to get your dose of healthy fats.

	DAY 1	DAY 2	DAY 3	DAY 4	DAY 5	DAY 6	DAY 7
Wake up	10 Minute Gingery Spinach with Cherries (75.9)	Quick and Healthy Cilantro Cucumber Detox Juice (76.9)	Blueberry Celery and Spinach Power Juice (72.9)	Apple Radish and Spinach Juice with Carrots (69.9)	Lemony Kale and Cucumber Beet Juice (84.9)	Tangy Celery Grapefruit Boost Drink (43.9)	Easy Cucumber Broccoli and Celery Juice (41.9)
Breakfast	Cherry Spinach and Ginger Drink (75.9)	Minty Lettuce Pineapple Juice with Coconut (70.9)	Anti-Aging Spinach and Artichoke Juice (74.9)	Cilantro Chard and Gingered Beet Juice (75.9)	Vitamin C Boosted Green Juice (80.9)	Green Tea Flax Seed and Spinach Juice (65.9)	10-minute Lettuce and Carrots Salad Juice (23.9)
Lunch	Clementine Lemon and Carrots Juice (75.9)	Cucumber Cilantro with Pineapple Spinach (86.9)	Maca Blueberry and Cinnamon Juice (94.9)	10 Minute Grapefruit and Celery Juice (70.9)	Lemony Kale and Cucumber Beet Juice (84.9)	Tangy Celery Grapefruit Boost Drink (43.9)	Watermelon and Cauliflower Celery Juice (57.9)
Afternoon snack	10 Minute Gingery Spinach with Cherries (75.9)	Quick and Healthy Cilantro Cucumber Detox Juice (76.9)	Blueberry Celery and Spinach Power Juice (72.9)	Lemony Green Beans and Spinach Juice (101)	Cucumber Orange Green Juice (71.9)	Spinach Cilantro and Lettuce Juice (86.9)	Easy Cucumber Broccoli and Celery Juice (41.9)
Dinner	Minty Carrot Cucumber Gingered Juice (93.9)	Limey Kale and Watermelon Juice (89.9)	Maca Blueberry and Cinnamon Juice (94.9)	Cilantro Chard and Gingered Beet Juice (75.9)	Vitamin C Boosted Green Juice (80.9)	Green Tea Flax Seed and Spinach Juice (65.9)	Lemony Apple Lettuce Cucumber Juice (62.9)
Dessert	Clementine Lemon and Carrots Juice (75.9)	Green Tea and Orange Juice with Parsley (60.9)	Sweet Potato and Zucchini Detox Juice (56.9)	10 Minute Grapefruit and Celery Juice (70.9)	Lemony Kale and Cucumber Beet Juice (84.9)	Tangy Celery Grapefruit Boost Drink (43.9)	Watermelon and Cauliflower Celery Juice (57.9)

Bedtime	Minty Carrot Cucumber Gingered Juice (93.9)	Limey Kale and Watermelon Juice (89.9)	Apple Artichoke and Celery Juice (74.9)	Apple Radish and Spinach Juice with Carrots (69.9)	Cucumber Orange Green Juice (71.9)	Spinach Cilantro and Lettuce Juice (86.9)	10-minute Lettuce and Carrots Salad Juice (23.9)
Total calories	567.3	552.3	542.3	534.4	475.4	437.3	310.3

CONCLUSION

Juicing can be exciting, most especially if you're doing it for weight loss and you start seeing results. There is a thing as too much though, and as much as it is healthy, exclusive juicing for long periods is harmful to health.

Where does too much start? Well, you should not juice exclusively for more than 5 days. All your meal plans for juicing exclusively should end at day 5 and if you intend to juice for long periods, what you need to do is to alternate 5 days of exclusive juicing and 5 days of regular eating in order to get maximum health and weight loss benefits. It is also important to get medical guidance from your doctor or nutritionist because everyone is built different and the number of calories the body needs are different. If you choose to make juicing a lifestyle and don't need to use a recipe book all the time, do not forget that exclusive juicing should not be done for more than 5 days.

Chapter 3
Start Your Day Green

10 Minute Clementine and Celery Juice

Prep time: 10 minutes | **Cook time:** 0 minutes | **Serves 2**

1 large bunch celery

2 clementine oranges

1. Wash all the ingredients.
2. Trim ends from the celery, then cut into 4-inch pieces.
3. Peel the clementine and separate into quarters.
4. Place a pitcher under the juicer's spout to collect the juice.
5. Feed the celery, then the clementine through the juicer's intake tube.
6. When the juice stops flowing, remove the pitcher and stir the juice.
7. Serve immediately.

PER SERVING

Calories: 95.9| Total Fat: 0.9g| Sugar: 15.9g| Carbohydrates: 27.9g| Fiber: 1.9g| Protein: 5g

Quick and Simple Green Juice

Prep time: 10 minutes | **Cook time:** 0 minutes | **Serves 2**

4 romaine lettuce leaves

4 celery ribs

1 green apple

1. Wash all the ingredients.
2. Trim the ends from the celery, then and cut into 4-inch pieces.
3. Remove the apple core and discard. Cut the apple into quarters, leaving the peel intact.
4. Place a pitcher under the juicer's spout to collect the juice.
5. Feed each ingredient through the juicer's intake tube in the order listed.
6. When the juice stops flowing, remove the pitcher and stir the juice.
7. Serve immediately.

PER SERVING

Calories: 72.9| Total Fat: 0.9g| Sugar: 14.9g| Carbohydrates: 22.9g| Fiber: 0.9g| Protein: 1.9g

Lemony Lettuce Beet Sunrise Special Drink

Prep time: 10 minutes | Cook time: 0 minutes | Serves 2

2 cups romaine lettuce (about 4 leaves)
2 tablespoons parsley leaves
½ green apple
½ beet
1 lemon

1. Wash all the ingredients.
2. Remove the apple core and discard. Cut the apple into quarters, leaving the peel intact.
3. Remove any greens from the beet and save for juicing later. Cut the beet into quarters.
4. Peel the lemon and cut into quarters.
5. Place a pitcher under the juicer's spout to collect the juice.
6. Feed each ingredient through the juicer's intake tube in the order listed.
7. When the juice stops flowing, remove the pitcher and stir the juice.
8. Serve immediately.

PER SERVING

Calories: 62.9| Total Fat: 0.9g| Sugar: 11.9g| Carbohydrates: 20.9g| Fiber: 0.9g| Protein: 2.9g

Minty Chi Spinach and Apple Juice

Prep time: 10 minutes | Cook time: 0 minutes | Serves 2

3 cups spinach
10 mint leaves
1 green apple
1 teaspoon chia seeds

1. Wash all the spinach, mint leaves, and apple.
2. Remove the apple core and discard. Cut the apple into quarters, leaving the peel intact.
3. Place a pitcher under the juicer's spout to collect the juice.
4. Feed the first three ingredients through the juicer's intake tube in the order listed.
5. When the juice stops flowing, remove the pitcher, add the chia seeds, stir the juice, and let sit for five minutes.
6. Serve immediately.

PER SERVING

Calories: 73.9| Total Fat: 0.9g| Sugar: 12.9g| Carbohydrates: 20.9g| Fiber: 0.9g| Protein: 2.9g3

Grapefruits Plus Peas and Carrots Juice

Prep time: 5 minutes | Cook time: 0 minutes | Serves 1

2 grapefruits, peeled
1 red bell pepper
2 pears
6 carrots

1. Thoroughly wash the carrots, pears and grapefruits, peel and cut into chunks. Throw into a juicer along with red pepper.
2. Process and drink immediately.

PER SERVING

Calories: 89.9 | Fat: 1.9g | Protein: 0.9g | Carbohydrates: 18.9g | Sugar: 4.9mg

5 Minute Honey Strawberry Lemonade

Prep time: 5 minutes | Cook time: 0 minutes | Serves 4

1 cup strawberries
3 lemons
3 cups cold water
1 tablespoon raw honey (optional)

1. Peel, cut, deseed, and/or chop the ingredients as needed.
2. Place a container under the juicer's spout.
3. Feed the strawberries and lemons through the juicer.
4. Stir the water and honey into the juice and pour into glasses to serve.

PER SERVING

Calories: 34.9 | Fat: 0g | Protein: 0g | Carbohydrates: 9.9g | Sugar: 3.9mg

Easy Banana Berry Cilantro Juice

Prep time: 5 minutes | Cook time: 0 minutes | Serves 2

2 cups strawberries
1 cup cilantro
1 cup cold water
1 small banana

1. Peel, cut, deseed, and/or chop the ingredients as needed.
2. Place a container under the juicer's spout.
3. Feed the strawberries and cilantro through the juicer.
4. In a blender, combine the water and banana and blend until smooth.
5. Add the strawberry cilantro juice and pulse to blend.
6. Pour into glasses and serve.

PER SERVING

Calories: 91.9| Fat: 0.9g | Protein: 1.9g | Carbohydrates: 22.9g | Sugar: 7.9mg

Quick Juicy Apple and Ginger Beets

Prep time: 5 minutes | Cook time: 0 minutes | Serves 2

2 medium beets
2 large carrots
1 medium apple
1 cup cold water
1-inch piece gingerroot

1. 1. In a blender, combine all the ingredients and blend until as smooth as possible.
2. 2. Press the mixture through a fine mesh strainer until all the juice is out.
3. 3. Discard the pulp, pour into glasses, and serve.

PER SERVING

Calories: 76.9| Fat: 0g | Protein: 0.9g | Carbohydrates: 18.9g | Sugar: 12.9mg

Easy Cucumber Broccoli and Celery Juice

Prep time: 5 minutes | Cook time: 0 minutes | Serves 2

2 large stalks celery
1 small head broccoli
1 cucumber
1 small pear
½ bunch parsley leaves

1. Peel, cut, deseed, and/or chop the ingredients as needed.
2. Place a container under the juicer's spout.
3. Feed the ingredients one at a time, in the order listed, through the juicer.
4. Stir the juice and pour into glasses to serve.

PER SERVING

Calories: 41.9| Fat: 0g | Protein: 0.9g | Carbohydrates: 8.9g | Sugar: 5.9mg

Apple Radish and Spinach Juice with Carrots

Prep time: 5 minutes | Cook time: 0 minutes | Serves 2

8 small radishes with greens
2 cups baby spinach leaves
1 large carrot
1 large stalk celery
1 medium apple
½-inch piece gingerroot

1. Peel, cut, deseed, and/or chop the ingredients as needed.
2. Place a container under the juicer's spout.
3. Feed the ingredients one at a time, in the order listed, through the juicer.
4. Stir the juice and pour into glasses to serve.

PER SERVING

Calories: 69.9| Fat: 0g | Protein: 0.9g | Carbohydrates: 16.9g | Sugar: 10.9mg

Cucumber and Kale Blended with Spinach

Prep time: 5 minutes | Cook time: 0 minutes | Serves 2

1 cup baby spinach leaves
1 large carrot
1 large stalk celery
½ bunch kale leaves
½ small cucumber
1 medium apple
1-inch piece gingerroot

1. Peel, cut, deseed, and/or chop the ingredients as needed.
2. Place a container under the juicer's spout.
3. Feed the ingredients one at a time, in the order listed, through the juicer.
4. Stir the juice and pour into glasses to serve.

PER SERVING

Calories: 71.9| Fat: 0g | Protein: 0.9g | Carbohydrates: 16.9g | Sugar: 11.mg

10 Minute Lettuce and Carrot Juice

Prep time: 10 minutes | Cook time: 0 minutes | Serves 2

2 large stalks celery
1 large carrot
½ romaine lettuce heart
½ medium cucumber
3 sprigs cilantro

1. Peel, cut, deseed, and/or chop the ingredients as needed.
2. Place a container under the juicer's spout.
3. Feed the ingredients one at a time, in the order listed, through the juicer.
4. Stir the juice and pour into glasses to serve.

PER SERVING

Calories: 23.9| Fat: 0g | Protein: 0.9g | Carbohydrates: 4.9g | Sugar: 2.9mg

Quick Kale Cucumber and Celery Juice
Prep time: 5 minutes | Cook time: 0 minutes | Serves 2

10 kale leaves
2 cucumbers
6 celery sticks
2 pears

1. Peel, cut, deseed, and/or chop the ingredients as needed.
2. Place a container under the juicer's spout.
3. Feed the first four ingredients one at a time, in the order listed, through the juicer.
4. Stir the juice and pour into glasses to serve.

PER SERVING
Calories: 23.9| Fat: 0g | Protein: 0.9g | Carbohydrates: 3.9g | Sugar: 2.9mg

5 Minute Pear and Celery Juice
Prep time: 5 minutes | Cook time: 0 minutes | Serves 1

3 celery roots
2 pears

1. Peel, cut, deseed, and/or chop the ingredients as needed.
2. Place a container under the juicer's spout.
3. Feed the ingredients in the order listed, through the juicer.
4. Stir the juice and pour into glasses to serve.

PER SERVING
Calories: 56.9| Fat: 0g | Protein: 0.9g | Carbohydrates: 14.9g | Sugar: 9.5mg

Gingery Fennel Spinach and Celery Juice

Prep time: 10 minutes | Cook time: 0 minutes | Serves 1

2 handfuls of spinach
2 granny smith apples
1 pear, pitted
1 fennel
1 mango
1 celery stalk
½ thumb size piece of ginger

1. Wash all ingredients and process through a juicer.
2. Pour the extracted juice into a glass, stir well and drink immediately.

PER SERVING

Calories: 97.9| Fat: 0g | Protein: 0.9g | Carbohydrates: 22.9g | Sugar: 15.9mg

Beet Cabbage Green Juice with Pineapple

Prep time: 5 minutes | Cook time: 0 minutes | Serves 1

1 medium beet, peeled
2 leaves of red cabbage
3 medium carrots
½ lemon, peeled
1 orange, peeled
½ pineapple
2 handfuls of spinach

1. Peel the pineapple, beet, orange and citrus and process through a juicer along with spinach, carrots, and cabbage leaves.
2. Pour the extracted juice into a glass and enjoy.

PER SERVING

Calories: 56.9| Fat: 0g | Protein: 0.9g | Carbohydrates: 14.9g | Sugar: 9.5mg

5 Minute Tangy Kale Celery Juice

Prep time: 5 minutes | Cook time: 0 minutes | Serves 1

1 bunch kale
1 bunch celery
1 lemon

1. Wash the celery kale and lemon and run through a juicer.
2. Drink immediately.

PER SERVING

Calories: 22.9| Fat: 0g | Protein: 0.9g | Carbohydrates: 4.9g | Sugar: 0.9mg

Lemony Cabbage Celery Green Juice

Prep time: 5 minutes | Cook time: 0 minutes | Serves 1

½ head green or Napa cabbage
1 bunch dandelion greens
½ bunch celery
½ lemon, unpeeled
1-inch knob of fresh ginger root

1. Process the cabbage, celery, dandelion greens, lemon, and ginger through a juicer.
2. Add little honey to provide the juice some sweetness.

PER SERVING

Calories: 46.9| Fat: 0g | Protein: 1.9g | Carbohydrates: 10.9g | Sugar: 5.9mg

5 Minute Fruity Juice with Spinach
Prep time: 5 minutes | Cook time: 0 minutes | Serves 2

1 bunch spinach leaves
1 medium apple
1 medium pear
1 medium navel orange

1. Peel, cut, deseed, and/or chop the ingredients as needed.
2. Place a container under the juicer's spout.
3. Feed the ingredients one at a time, in the order listed, through the juicer.
4. Stir the juice and pour into glasses to serve.

PER SERVING

Calories: 85.9| Fat: 0g | Protein: 5.9g | Carbohydrates: 18.9g | Sugar: 9.9mg

Mango Kale and Spinach Celery Juice
Prep time: 5 minutes | Cook time: 0 minutes | Serves 2

4 large kale leaves
3 large stalks celery
1 ripe mango
1 small bunch spinach leaves

1. Peel, cut, deseed, and/or chop the ingredients as needed.
2. Place a container under the juicer's spout.
3. Feed the ingredients one at a time, in the order listed, through the juicer.
4. Stir the juice and pour into glasses to serve.

PER SERVING

Calories: 85.9 Fat: 0.9g | Protein: 9.9g | Carbohydrates: 12.9g | Sugar: 1.9mg

Zucchini Plus Broccoli and Kale Juice

Prep time: 5 minutes | Cook time: 0 minutes | Serves 1

½ head broccoli
4 leaves kale
½ green bell pepper
1 zucchini, peeled
1 green apple

1. Wash the pepper, broccoli, zucchini, kale, and apple and cut into chunks.
2. Then pass all ingredients through a juicer.
3. Pour the juice into a glass and drink immediately.

PER SERVING

Calories: 52.9| Fat: 0g | Protein: 0.9g | Carbohydrates: 13.9g | Sugar: 9.9mg

5 Minute Honeydew and Asparagus Lemonade

Prep time: 5 minutes | Cook time: 0 minutes | Serves 2

1 small honeydew melon
1 bunch asparagus
1 medium pear
1 lemon

1. Peel, cut, deseed, and/or chop the ingredients as needed.
2. Place a container under the juicer's spout.
3. Feed the ingredients one at a time, in the order listed, through the juicer.
4. Stir the juice and pour into glasses to serve.

PER SERVING

Calories: 33.9| Fat: 0g | Protein: 0g | Carbohydrates: 8.9g | Sugar: 5.9mg

Easy and Quick Lettuce Celery Juice
Prep time: 5 minutes | Cook time: 0 minutes | Serves 1

4 romaine lettuce leaves
4 celery ribs
1 green apple

1. Wash all the ingredients.
2. Trim the ends from the celery, then and cut into 4-inch pieces.
3. Remove the apple core and discard. Cut the apple into quarters, leaving the peel intact.
4. Place a pitcher under the juicer's spout to collect the juice.
5. Feed each ingredient through the juicer's intake tube in the order listed.
6. When the juice stops flowing, remove the pitcher and stir the juice.
7. Serve immediately.

PER SERVING

Calories: 72.9| Fat: 0.9g | Protein: 1.9g | Carbohydrates: 22.9g | Sugar: 7.9mg

Tangy Romaine Lettuce and Beet
Prep time: 5 minutes | Cook time: 0 minutes | Serves 1

2 cups romaine lettuce (about 4 leaves)
2 tablespoons parsley leaves
½ green apple
½ beet
1 lemon

1. Wash all the ingredients.
2. Remove the apple core and discard. Cut the apple into quarters, leaving the peel intact.
3. Remove any greens from the beet and save for juicing later. Cut the beet into quarters.
4. Peel the lemon and cut into quarters.
5. Place a pitcher under the juicer's spout to collect the juice.
6. Feed each ingredient through the juicer's intake tube in the order listed.
7. When the juice stops flowing, remove the pitcher and stir the juice.
8. Serve immediately.

PER SERVING

Calories: 62.9| Fat: 0.9g | Protein: 2.9g | Carbohydrates: 20.9g | Sugar: 11.9mg

Apple Chia and Spinach with Mint

Prep time: 5 minutes | Cook time: 0 minutes | Serves 1

3 cups spinach
10 mint leaves
1 green apple
1 teaspoon chia seeds

1. Wash all the spinach, mint leaves, and apple.
2. Remove the apple core and discard. Cut the apple into quarters, leaving the peel intact.
3. Place a pitcher under the juicer's spout to collect the juice.
4. Feed the first three ingredients through the juicer's intake tube in the order listed.
5. When the juice stops flowing, remove the pitcher, add the chia seeds, stir the juice, and let sit for five minutes.
6. Serve immediately.

PER SERVING

Calories: 73.9| Fat: 0.9g | Protein: 2.9g | Carbohydrates: 20.9g | Sugar: 12.9mg

Lemony Carrots and Pepper Lettuce Juice

Prep time: 5 minutes | Cook time: 0 minutes | Serves 1

3 carrots
6 romaine lettuce leaves
2 medium tomatoes
2 green onions
½ green bell pepper
¼ cup parsley
½ lemon

1. Wash all the ingredients.
2. Trim the ends from carrots and green onions, then cut into 4-inch pieces.
3. Remove the stems from the tomatoes and cut into quarters.
4. Remove the stem and seeds from the bell pepper. Cut into small pieces.
5. Peel the lemon half and cut into quarters.
6. Place a pitcher under the juicer's spout to collect the juice.
7. Feed each ingredient through the juicer's intake tube in the order listed.
8. When the juice stops flowing, remove the pitcher and stir the juice.
9. Serve immediately.

PER SERVING

Calories: 88.9| Fat: 0.9g | Protein: 4.9g | Carbohydrates: 27.9g | Sugar: 13.9mg

5 Minute Lettuce Sprouts Celery Juice
Prep time: 5 minutes | Cook time: 0 minutes | Serves 1

4 celery ribs
1 cucumber
8 lettuce leaves
½ cup alfalfa sprouts

1. Wash all the ingredients.
2. Trim the ends from the celery and cucumber, then cut into 4-inch pieces.
3. Place a pitcher under the juicer's spout to collect the juice.
4. Feed each ingredient through the juicer's intake tube in the order listed.
5. When the juice stops flowing, remove the pitcher and stir the juice.
6. Serve immediately.

PER SERVING

Calories: 54.9| Fat: 0.9g | Protein: 4.9g | Carbohydrates: 15.9g | Sugar: 6.5mg

Kale Grapefruit and Cucumber Juice
Prep time: 10 minutes | Cook time: 0 minutes | Serves 2

1 large celery stalk
2 kale leaves
½ pink or red grapefruit, peeled
1 Cara Cara or other small orange, peeled
½ cup pineapple
½ cucumber

1. Peel, cut, deseed, and/or chop the ingredients as needed.
2. Place a container under the juicer's spout.
3. Feed the ingredients one at a time, in the order listed, through the juicer.
4. Stir the juice and pour into glasses to serve.

PER SERVING

Calories: 64.9| Fat: 0g | Protein: 0.9g | Carbohydrates: 15.9g | Sugar: 13.9mg

Sweet Potato and Peppered Broccoli with Celery
Prep time: 5 minutes | Cook time: 0 minutes | Serves 2

2-inch piece broccoli stem
4 large celery stalks
1 small sweet potato, peeled
½ lemon
1-inch piece fresh turmeric root
3 small oranges, peeled
Freshly ground black pepper (optional)

1. Place a container under the juicer's spout.
2. Feed the ingredients one at a time, in the order listed, through the juicer.
3. Stir the black pepper (if using) directly into the juice to increase your absorption of the curcumin in the turmeric.

PER SERVING

Calories: 34.9| Fat: 0g | Protein: 0.9g | Carbohydrates: 7.9g | Sugar: 2.9mg

Chapter 4
Immune Boosting Juices

Cherry Spinach and Ginger Drink

Prep time: 15 minutes | Cook time: 0 minutes | Serves 1

1½ cups spinach
1 cup cherries
Fresh ginger root
1 cup sparkling water

1. Wash the spinach, cherries, and ginger root.
2. Remove the cherry pits and stems.
3. Slice off a 2-inch piece of the ginger root.
4. Place a pitcher under the juicer's spout to collect the juice.
5. Feed each ingredient through the juicer's intake tube in the order listed.
6. When the juice stops flowing, remove the pitcher and stir the juice.
7. Serve immediately.

PER SERVING

Calories: 75.9| Fat: 0g | Protein: 1.9g | Carbohydrates: 20.9g | Sugar: 13.9g

Aloe Sprout and Cabbage Juice

Prep time: 10 minutes | Cook time: 0 minutes | Serves 1

¼ cup alfalfa sprouts
1 pear
1 cup cabbage
¼ cup aloe vera juice

1. Wash the alfalfa sprouts, pear, and cabbage.
2. Cut the pear into quarters, removing the core and seeds, but leaving the peel intact.
3. Cut the cabbage in half, then slice or chop into smaller pieces.
4. Place a pitcher under the juicer's spout to collect the juice.
5. Feed the first three ingredients through the juicer's intake tube in the order listed.
6. When the juice stops flowing, remove the pitcher, add the aloe vera juice, and stir.
7. Serve immediately.

PER SERVING

Calories: 90.9| Fat: 0g | Protein: 2.9g | Carbohydrates: 28.9g | Sugar: 16.9g

Peppered Broccoli Cucumber and Green Leaves

Prep time: 15 minutes | Cook time: 0 minutes | Serves 1

1 orange
½ red bell pepper
1 cup broccoli
2 collard green leaves
¼ cucumber

1. Wash all the ingredients.
2. Peel the orange and cut into quarters.
3. Remove the stem and seeds from the bell pepper. Cut into small pieces.
4. Remove the stalk from the broccoli crown with a knife and discard or save to juice later. Cut the crown into small florets.
5. Trim the ends from the cucumber, then cut into quarters.
6. Place a pitcher under the juicer's spout to collect the juice.
7. Feed each ingredient through the juicer's intake tube in the order listed.
8. When the juice stops flowing, remove the pitcher and stir the juice.
9. Serve immediately.

PER SERVING

Calories: 80.9| Fat: 0.9g | Protein: 3.9g | Carbohydrates: 23.9g | Sugar: 14.9g

Spinach Carrots and Celery Juice

Prep time: 15 minutes | Cook time: 0 minutes | Serves 1

2 cups spinach
3 cups broccoli
4 celery ribs
2 carrots

1. Wash all the ingredients.
2. Remove the stalk from the broccoli crown with a knife and discard or save to juice later. Cut the crown into small florets.
3. Trim the ends from the celery and carrots, then cut into 4-inch pieces.
4. Place a pitcher under the juicer's spout to collect the juice.
5. Feed each ingredient through the juicer's intake tube in the order listed.
6. When the juice stops flowing, remove the pitcher and stir the juice.
7. Serve immediately.

PER SERVING

Calories: 68.9| Fat: 0.9g | Protein: 5.9g | Carbohydrates: 19.9g | Sugar: 6.9g

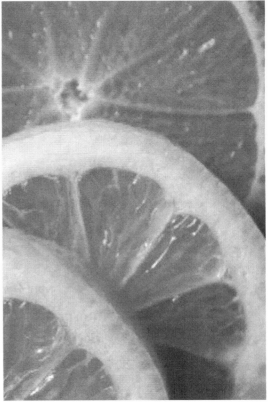

Immune Support Carrot and Orange Juice

Prep time: 15 minutes | Cook time: 0 minutes | Serves 2

3 medium carrots
2 small oranges, peeled

1. Peel, cut, deseed, and/or chop the ingredients as needed.
2. Place a container under the juicer's spout.
3. Feed the ingredients one at a time, in the order listed, through the juicer.
4. Stir the juice and pour into glasses to serve.

PER SERVING

Calories: 74.9| Fat: 0.9g | Protein: 1.9g | Carbohydrates: 17.9g | Sugar: 8.9g

Quick and Healthy Carrots Cantaloupe Juice

Prep time: 10 minutes | Cook time: 0 minutes | Serves 2

4 medium carrots
1 cup cantaloupe

1. Peel, cut, deseed, and/or chop the ingredients as needed.
2. Place a container under the juicer's spout.
3. Feed the ingredients one at a time, in the order listed, through the juicer.
4. Stir the juice and pour into glasses to serve.

PER SERVING

Calories: 79.9| Fat: 0.9g | Protein: 1.9g | Carbohydrates: 18.9g | Sugar: 12.9g

10 Minute Grapefruit and Celery Juice
Prep time: 10 minutes | Cook time: 0 minutes | Serves 2

2 large celery stalks
4 large romaine leaves
1 pink or red grapefruit, peeled

1. Peel, cut, deseed, and/or chop the ingredients as needed.
2. Place a container under the juicer's spout.
3. Feed the ingredients one at a time, in the order listed, through the juicer.
4. Stir the juice and pour into glasses to serve.

PER SERVING

Calories: 70.9| Fat: 0.9g | Protein: 4.9g | Carbohydrates: 13.9g | Sugar: 8.9g

Watermelon and Cauliflower Celery Juice

Prep time: 5 minutes | Cook time: 0 minutes | Serves 2

½ cup cauliflower
4 large celery stalks
2 cups watermelon

1. Peel, cut, deseed, and/or chop the ingredients as needed.
2. Place a container under the juicer's spout.
3. Feed the ingredients one at a time, in the order listed, through the juicer.
4. Stir the juice and pour into glasses to serve.

PER SERVING

Calories: 57.9| Fat: 0.9g | Protein: 1.9g | Carbohydrates: 13.9g | Sugar: 10.9g

Yellow Peppers Blended with Limey Spinach

Prep time: 10 minutes | Cook time: 0 minutes | Serves 2

2 large yellow bell peppers
4 cups spinach
1 lemon
½ large cucumber

1. Peel, cut, deseed, and/or chop the ingredients as needed.
2. Place a container under the juicer's spout.
3. Feed the ingredients one at a time, in the order listed, through the juicer.
4. Stir the juice and pour into glasses to serve.

PER SERVING

Calories: 44.9| Fat: 0.9g | Protein: 2.9g | Carbohydrates: 9.9g | Sugar: 3.9g

Quick Ginger Celery Pepper Shot

Prep time: 5 minutes | Cook time: 0 minutes | Serves 2

½- to 1-inch piece fresh ginger root
¼ large yellow bell pepper
¼ lemon
2-inch piece celery

1. Peel, cut, deseed, and/or chop the ingredients as needed.
2. Place a container under the juicer's spout.
3. Feed the ingredients one at a time, in the order listed, through the juicer.
4. Stir the juice and pour into glasses to serve.

PER SERVING

Calories: 3.9| Fat: 0g | Protein: 0g | Carbohydrates: 0.9g | Sugar: 0.9g

Tangy Celery Grapefruit Boost Drink

Prep time: 5 minutes | Cook time: 0 minutes | Serves 3

2 large yellow bell peppers
1 large celery stalk
1 lemon
1-inch piece fresh ginger root
1 pink or red grapefruit, peeled

1. Peel, cut, deseed, and/or chop the ingredients as needed.
2. Place a container under the juicer's spout.
3. Feed the ingredients one at a time, in the order listed, through the juicer.
4. Stir the juice and pour into glasses to serve.

PER SERVING

Calories: 43.9| Fat: 0g | Protein: 0.9g | Carbohydrates: 10.9g | Sugar: 7.9g

Healthy Asparagus Cucumber and Kale Salad

Prep time: 5 minutes | Cook time: 0 minutes | Serves 2

8 asparagus spears
½ lemon
4 medium kale leaves
4 small carrots
8 small celery stalks
1 large cucumber

1. Peel, cut, deseed, and/or chop the ingredients as needed.
2. Place a container under the juicer's spout.
3. Feed the ingredients one at a time, in the order listed, through the juicer.
4. Stir the juice and pour into glasses to serve.

PER SERVING

Calories: 89.9| Fat: 0.9g | Protein: 3.9g | Carbohydrates: 18.9g | Sugar: 8.9g

Ginger Beet and Tangy Celery Juice

Prep time: 5 minutes | Cook time: 0 minutes | Serves 2

1 medium golden or red beet
1 large yellow bell pepper
1-inch piece fresh ginger root
½ lemon
8 small celery stalks
½ large cucumber

1. Peel, cut, deseed, and/or chop the ingredients as needed.
2. Place a container under the juicer's spout.
3. Feed the ingredients one at a time, in the order listed, through the juicer.
4. Stir the juice and pour into glasses to serve.

PER SERVING

Calories: 48.9| Fat: 0.9g | Protein: 1.9g | Carbohydrates: 10.9g | Sugar: 5.9g

Asparagus Blended with Peppered Chard

Prep time: 5 minutes | Cook time: 0 minutes | Serves 2

8 asparagus spears
2 cups Swiss chard
½ lemon
1 orange, peeled
½ yellow bell pepper
1 large cucumber

1. Peel, cut, deseed, and/or chop the ingredients as needed.
2. Place a container under the juicer's spout.
3. Feed the ingredients one at a time, in the order listed, through the juicer.
4. Stir the juice and pour into glasses to serve.

PER SERVING

Calories: 83.9| Fat: 0.9g | Protein: 2.9g | Carbohydrates: 18.9g | Sugar: 47.9

Quick and Healthy Carrot Celery Juice

Prep time: 5 minutes | Cook time: 0 minutes | Serves 2

4 large carrots
½ lemon
6 large celery stalks

1. Peel, cut, deseed, and/or chop the ingredients as needed.
2. Place a container under the juicer's spout.
3. Feed the ingredients one at a time, in the order listed, through the juicer.
4. Stir the juice and pour into glasses to serve.

PER SERVING

Calories: 69.0| Fat: 0.9g | Protein: 1.9g | Carbohydrates: 15.9g | Sugar: 7.9g

Tangy Celery and Chard with Pear

Prep time: 5 minutes | Cook time: 0 minutes | Serves 2

4 small celery stalks
4 small Swiss chard leaves
1 firm pear
½ lemon
½ large cucumber

1. Peel, cut, deseed, and/or chop the ingredients as needed.
2. Place a container under the juicer's spout.
3. Feed the ingredients one at a time, in the order listed, through the juicer.
4. Stir the juice and pour into glasses to serve.

PER SERVING

Calories: 59.9| Fat: 0.9g | Protein: 2.9g | Carbohydrates: 13.9g | Sugar: 6.9g

10 Minute Healthy Ulcer Care Drink

Prep time: 10 minutes | Cook time: 0 minutes | Serves 2

2 cups green cabbage
2 cups spinach
3 green chard leaves
3 celery ribs
1 green apple

1. Wash all the ingredients.
2. Cut the cabbage in half, then slice or chop into smaller pieces.
3. Trim the ends from the celery, then cut into 4-inch pieces.
4. Remove the apple core and discard. Cut the apple into quarters, leaving the peel intact.
5. Place a pitcher under the juicer's spout to collect the juice.
6. Feed each ingredient through the juicer's intake tube in the order listed.
7. When the juice stops flowing, remove the pitcher and stir the juice.
8. Serve immediately.

PER SERVING

Calories: 87.9| Total Fat: 0.9g| Sugar: 15.9g| Carbohydrates: 27.9g| Fiber: 0.9g| Protein: 4.9g

Quick and Healthy Cilantro Cucumber Detox Juice

Prep time: 10 minutes | Cook time: 0 minutes | Serves 2

1 cucumber
1 bunch cilantro
5 celery ribs
2 lemons

1. Wash all the ingredients.
2. Trim the ends from the cucumber and celery, then cut into 4-inch pieces.
3. Peel the lemons and cut into quarters.
4. Place a pitcher under the juicer's spout to collect the juice.
5. Feed each ingredient through the juicer's intake tube in the order listed.
6. When the juice stops flowing, remove the pitcher and stir the juice.
7. Serve immediately.

PER SERVING

Calories: 76.9| Total Fat: 0.9g| Sugar: 9.9g| Carbohydrates: 27.9g| Fiber: 0.9g| Protein: 4.9g

10 Minute Gingery Spinach with Cherries

Prep time: 10 minutes | Cook time: 0 minutes | Serves 2

1½ cups spinach
1 cup cherries
Fresh ginger root
1 cup sparkling water

1. Wash the spinach, cherries, and ginger root.
2. Remove the cherry pits and stems.
3. Slice off a 2-inch piece of the ginger root.
4. Place a pitcher under the juicer's spout to collect the juice.
5. Feed each ingredient through the juicer's intake tube in the order listed.
6. When the juice stops flowing, remove the pitcher and stir the juice.
7. Serve immediately.

PER SERVING

Calories: 75.9| Total Fat: 0g| Sugar: 13.9g| Carbohydrates: 20.9g| Fiber: 0.9g| Protein: 1.9g

Aloe Vera and Cabbage Cleanser

Prep time: 10 minutes | Cook time: 0 minutes | Serves 2

¼ cup alfalfa sprouts
1 pear
1 cup cabbage
¼ cup aloe vera juice

1. Wash the alfalfa sprouts, pear, and cabbage.
2. Cut the pear into quarters, removing the core and seeds, but leaving the peel intact.
3. Cut the cabbage in half, then slice or chop into smaller pieces.
4. Place a pitcher under the juicer's spout to collect the juice.
5. Feed the first three ingredients through the juicer's intake tube in the order listed.
6. When the juice stops flowing, remove the pitcher, add the aloe vera juice, and stir.
7. Serve immediately.

PER SERVING

Calories: 90.9| Total Fat: 0g| Sugar: 16.9g| Carbohydrates: 28.9g| Fiber: 7.9g| Protein: 2.9g

Vitamin C Boosted Green Juice

Prep time: 10 minutes | Cook time: 0 minutes | Serves 2

1 orange
½ red bell pepper
1 cup broccoli
2 collard green leaves
¼ cucumber

1. Wash all the ingredients.
2. Peel the orange and cut into quarters.
3. Remove the stem and seeds from the bell pepper. Cut into small pieces.
4. Remove the stalk from the broccoli crown with a knife and discard or save to juice later. Cut the crown into small florets.
5. Trim the ends from the cucumber, then cut into quarters.
6. Place a pitcher under the juicer's spout to collect the juice.
7. Feed each ingredient through the juicer's intake tube in the order listed.
8. When the juice stops flowing, remove the pitcher and stir the juice.
9. Serve immediately.

PER SERVING

Calories: 80.9| Total Fat: 0.9g| Sugar: 14.9g| Carbohydrates: 23.9g| Fiber: 0.9g| Protein: 3.9g

Celery Spinach and Carrots Healing Drink

Prep time: 10 minutes | Cook time: 0 minutes | Serves 2

2 cups spinach
3 cups broccoli
4 celery ribs
2 carrots

1. Wash all the ingredients.
2. Remove the stalk from the broccoli crown with a knife and discard or save to juice later. Cut the crown into small florets.
3. Trim the ends from the celery and carrots, then cut into 4-inch pieces.
4. Place a pitcher under the juicer's spout to collect the juice.
5. Feed each ingredient through the juicer's intake tube in the order listed.
6. When the juice stops flowing, remove the pitcher and stir the juice.
7. Serve immediately.

PER SERVING

Calories: 68.9| Total Fat: 0.9g| Sugar: 6.9g| Carbohydrates: 19.9g| Fiber: 0.9g| Protein: 5.9g

Chapter 5
Energize with Green

Blueberry Celery and Spinach Power Juice

Prep time: 10 minutes | Cook time: 0 minutes | Serves 2

2 cups spinach
6 celery ribs
1 cup blueberries
8 ounces coconut water

1. Wash the spinach, celery, and blueberries.
2. Trim the ends from the celery, then cut into 4-inch pieces.
3. Place a pitcher under the juicer's spout to collect the juice.
4. Feed the first three ingredients through the juicer's intake tube in the order listed.
5. When the juice stops flowing, remove the pitcher, add the coconut water, and stir.
6. Serve immediately.

PER SERVING

Calories: 72.9| Total Fat: 0.9g| Sugar: 12.9g| Carbohydrates: 20.9g| Fiber: 0.9g| Protein: 2.9g

Green Tea Flax Seed and Spinach Juice

Prep time: 10 minutes | Cook time: 0 minutes | Serves 2

¾ cup green tea
2 cups spinach
1 red apple
2 teaspoons ground flax seed

1. Brew the green tea and let it cool.
2. Wash the spinach and apple.
3. Remove the apple core and discard. Cut the apple into quarters, leaving the peel intact.
4. Place a pitcher under the juicer's spout to collect the juice.
5. Feed the spinach, then the apple through the juicer's intake tube.
6. When the juice stops flowing, remove the pitcher, add the green tea and flax seed, then stir.
7. Serve immediately.

PER SERVING

Calories: 65.9| Total Fat: 1.9g| Sugar: 10.9g| Carbohydrates: 16.9g| Fiber: 0.9g| Protein: 1.9g

Minty Carrot Cucumber Gingered Juice

Prep time: 10 minutes | Cook time: 0 minutes | Serves 2

2 cucumbers
3 carrots
2 tablespoons parsley
1 sprig mint leaves
Fresh ginger root

1. Wash all the ingredients.
2. Trim the ends from the cucumbers and carrots, then cut into 4-inch pieces.
3. Slice off a ½-inch piece of the ginger root.
4. Place a pitcher under the juicer's spout to collect the juice.
5. Feed each ingredient through the juicer's intake tube in the order listed.
6. When the juice stops flowing, remove the pitcher and stir the juice.
7. Serve immediately.

PER SERVING

Calories: 93.9| Total Fat: 9.9g| Sugar: 10.9g| Carbohydrates: 25.9g| Fiber: 0.9g| Protein: 3.9g

10 Minute Limey Celery and Cucumber

Prep time: 10 minutes | Cook time: 0 minutes | Serves 2

1 cucumber
1 romaine heart
4 celery ribs
1 lime
½ tablespoon wheatgrass powder

1. Wash the cucumber, romaine, celery, and lime.
2. Trim the ends from the cucumber and celery, then cut into 4-inch pieces.
3. Peel the lime and cut into quarters.
4. Place a pitcher under the juicer's spout to collect the juice.
5. Feed the first four ingredients through the juicer's intake tube in the order listed.
6. When the juice stops flowing, remove the pitcher, add the wheatgrass powder, and stir the juice.
7. Serve immediately.

PER SERVING

Calories: 97.9| Total Fat: 0.9g| Sugar: 7.9g| Carbohydrates: 25.9g| Fiber: 1.9g| Protein: 6.9g

Cilantro Chard and Gingered Beet Juice

Prep time: 10 minutes | Cook time: 0 minutes | Serves 2

1 cucumber
1 Swiss chard leaf
2 sprigs cilantro
½ small to medium size beet
3 celery ribs
½ lemon
Fresh ginger root

1. Wash all the ingredients.
2. Trim the ends from the cucumber and celery, then cut into 4-inch pieces.
3. Remove any greens from the beet and save for juicing later. Cut the beet into quarters.
4. Peel the lemon and cut into quarters.
5. Slice off a 1-inch piece of the ginger root.
6. Place a pitcher under the juicer's spout to collect the juice.
7. Feed each ingredient through the juicer's intake tube in the order listed.
8. When the juice stops flowing, remove the pitcher and stir the juice.
9. Serve immediately.

PER SERVING

Calories: 75.9 | Total Fat: 0.9g | Sugar: 9.9g | Carbohydrates: 21.9g | Fiber: 0.9g | Protein: 3.9g

Maca Blueberry and Cinnamon Juice

Prep time: 10 minutes | Cook time: 0 minutes | Serves 2

1 cup blueberries
2 cups spinach
1 cucumber
Fresh ginger root
½ teaspoon maca powder
¼ teaspoon cinnamon

1. Wash the blueberries, spinach, cucumber, and ginger root.
2. Trim the ends from the cucumber, then cut into 4-inch pieces.
3. Slice off a ½-inch piece of the ginger root.
4. Place a pitcher under the juicer's spout to collect the juice.
5. Feed the first four ingredients through the juicer's intake tube in the order listed.
6. When the juice stops flowing, remove the pitcher, add the maca powder and cinnamon, then stir.
7. Serve immediately.

PER SERVING

Calories: 94.9 | Total Fat: 0.9g | Sugar: 13.9g | Carbohydrates: 26.9g | Fiber: 0.9g | Protein: 3.9g

Chapter 6
Weight Loss Juices

Pineapple Jalapeno and Cilantro Juice

Prep time: 5 minutes | Cook time: 0 minutes | Serves 1

1 orange
¼ fresh pineapple
½ handful cilantro
½ small jalapeno, seeded

1. Peel the pineapple and orange and process through a juicer along with jalapeno and cilantro.
2. Pour the juice into a glass and enjoy.

PER SERVING

Calories: 70.9| Fat: 0g | Protein: 0.9g | Carbohydrates: 19.9g | Sugar: 14.9mg

Gingery Grapefruit and Orange Juice

Prep time: 5 minutes | Cook time: 0 minutes | Serves 1

1 ruby grapefruit
1 orange
2 carrots
½-inch (1 cm) piece of ginger

1. Wash and peel all ingredients.
2. Pass through a juicer and drink immediately.

PER SERVING

Calories: 24.9| Fat: 0g | Protein: 0g | Carbohydrates: 5.9g | Sugar: 2.9mg

Chilled Lemony Orange Juice with Cabbage

Prep time: 5 minutes | Cook time: 0 minutes | Serves 1

½ young cabbage
1 small carrot
3 oranges, peeled
½ lemon juice
a thumb size piece of ginger
Ice cubes

1. Run the carrot, ginger, cabbage, and oranges through a juicer.
2. Pour into a glass, add the lemon juice, stir well, and enjoy.

PER SERVING

Calories: 24.9| Fat: 0g | Protein: 0g | Carbohydrates: 5.9g | Sugar: 2.9mg

5 Minute Fruity Weight Loss Juice

Prep time: 5 minutes | Cook time: 0 minutes | Serves 1

4 rounds of pineapple
1 grapefruit (juice of 1 grapefruit)
1 cup of water

1. Peel the pineapple and slice into rounds.
2. Run through a juicer along with the grapefruit. Pour the juice into a tall glass, add 1 cup of water, stir well and drink immediately.

PER SERVING

Calories: 83.9| Fat: 0g | Protein: 1.9g | Carbohydrates: 20.9g | Sugar: 17.9mg3

Quite Lime and Grapefruit Juice

Prep time: 5 minutes | Cook time: 0 minutes | Serves 1

2 pink grapefruits
1 lime

1. Using a juicer or a citrus press, juice the grapefruits and lime.
2. Pour into a glass over ice and drink immediately.

PER SERVING

Calories: 86.9| Fat: 0g | Protein: 1.9g | Carbohydrates: 82.9g | Sugar: 21.9mg

Apple Cucumber and Spinach Detox Juice

Prep time: 5 minutes | Cook time: 0 minutes | Serves 2

1 green apple
1 cucumber
2 handfuls of spinach
1 handful of parsley
1 celery stick

1. Pass the cucumber along with spinach, parsley, celery, and apple through a juicer.
2. Pour into a glass over ice and serve immediately.

PER SERVING

Calories: 61.9| Fat: 0g | Protein: 0.9g | Carbohydrates: 14.9g | Sugar: 10.9mg

Minty Lettuce Pineapple Juice with Coconut

Prep time: 15 minutes | Cook time: 0 minutes | Serves 1

- 1 cup pineapple
- 4 large lettuce leaves
- 15 mint leaves
- ½ cup coconut water

1. Wash the lettuce and mint.
2. Trim the ends and skin from the pineapple, then remove the core and discard. Cut pineapple into 1-inch chunks.
3. Place a pitcher under the juicer's spout to collect the juice.
4. Feed the first three ingredients through the juicer's intake tube in the order listed.
5. When the juice stops flowing, remove the pitcher, add the coconut water, and stir.
6. Serve immediately.

PER SERVING

Calories: 70.9| Fat: 0.9g | Protein: 1.9g | Carbohydrates: 20.9g | Sugar: 13.9g

Cucumber Cilantro with Pineapple Spinach

Prep time: 15 minutes | Cook time: 0 minutes | Serves 1

1 cup pineapple
1 cup spinach
1 cup chopped lettuce leaves
1 cucumber
10 sprigs cilantro

1. Wash all the ingredients except the pineapple.
2. Trim the ends and skin from the pineapple, then remove the core and discard. Cut pineapple into 1-inch chunks.
3. Trim the ends from the cucumber, then cut into 4-inch pieces.
4. Place a pitcher under the juicer's spout to collect the juice.
5. Feed each ingredient through the juicer's intake tube in the order listed.
6. When the juice stops flowing, remove the pitcher and stir the juice.
7. Serve immediately.

PER SERVING

Calories: 86.9| Fat: 0.9g | Protein: 2.9g | Carbohydrates: 24.9g | Sugar: 14.9g

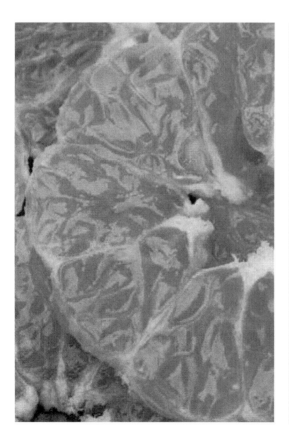

Green Tea and Orange Juice with Parsley

Prep time: 20 minutes | Cook time: 0 minutes | Serves 1

- ¾ cup green tea, cooled
- 10 dandelion greens
- 10 parsley sprigs
- 1 orange

1. Brew the green tea and let cool.
2. Wash the dandelion greens, parsley, and orange.
3. Peel the orange and separate into sections.
4. Place a pitcher under the juicer's spout to collect the juice.
5. Feed the dandelion greens, parsley, and orange through the juicer's intake tube in the order listed.
6. When the juice stops flowing, remove the pitcher, add the green tea to the juice, and stir.
7. Serve immediately.

PER SERVING

Calories: 60.9| Fat: 0.9g | Protein: 2.9g | Carbohydrates: 17.9g | Sugar: 8.9g

Lemony Apple Lettuce Cucumber Juice

Prep time: 20 minutes | Cook time: 0 minutes | Serves 1

½ cup water
1 teaspoon matcha powder
4 green lettuce leaves
½ cucumber
½ lemon
½ green apple

1. Heat the water to 180°F. Whisk in the matcha powder and let cool.
2. Wash the lettuce, cucumber, lemon, and apple.
3. Trim the ends from the cucumber, then cut into 4-inch pieces.
4. Peel the lemon and cut into quarters.
5. Remove the apple core and discard. Cut the apple into quarters, leaving the peel intact.
6. Place a pitcher under the juicer's spout to collect the juice.
7. Feed the lettuce, cucumber, lemon, and apple through the juicer's intake tube in the order listed.
8. When the juice stops flowing, remove the pitcher, add the matcha mixture, and stir.
9. Serve immediately.

PER SERVING

Calories: 62.9| Fat: 0g | Protein: 0.9g | Carbohydrates: 19.9g | Sugar: 12.9g

Asparagus Apple and Celery Juice

Prep time: 15 minutes | Cook time: 0 minutes | Serves 1

6 asparagus spears
1 green apple
2 celery ribs
¼ cup filtered water

1. Wash the asparagus, apple, and celery.
2. Trim ½ inch from the bottom of the asparagus, then cut stalks into 4-inch pieces.
3. Remove the apple core and discard. Cut the apple into quarters, leaving the peel intact.
4. Trim the ends from the celery, then cut into 4-inch pieces.
5. Place a pitcher under the juicer's spout to collect the juice.
6. Feed the asparagus, apple, and celery through the juicer's intake tube.
7. When the juice stops flowing, remove the pitcher, add the filtered water, and stir the juice.
8. Serve immediately.

PER SERVING

Calories: 60.9| Fat: 0g | Protein: 1.9g | Carbohydrates: 18.9g | Sugar: 12.9g

Limey Orange and Cucumber Juice

Prep time: 15 minutes | Cook time: 0 minutes | Serves 1

2 cups mixed greens
1 orange
1 cucumber
½ lime
1 teaspoon maca powder

1. Wash the mixed greens, orange, cucumber, and lime.
2. Peel the orange and lime, then cut into quarters.
3. Trim the ends from the cucumber, then cut into 4-inch pieces.
4. Place a pitcher under the juicer's spout to collect the juice.
5. Feed the first four ingredients through the juicer's intake tube in the order listed.
6. When the juice stops flowing, remove the pitcher, add the maca powder, and stir the juice.
7. Serve immediately.

PER SERVING

Calories: 71.9| Fat: 0g | Protein: 2.9g | Carbohydrates: 21.9g | Sugar: 12.9g

Gingered Kiwi Papaya and Coconut Water

Prep time: 10 minutes | Cook time: 0 minutes | Serves 2

1 medium kiwi, peeled
1 medium ripe papaya, peeled, seeded, cut
1 small pineapple, peeled, cored, and sliced
1 (1-inch) piece fresh ginger, peeled
½ cup fresh young coconut water

1. Peel and slice the papaya, pineapple, kiwi, and ginger. Process through a juicer.
2. Stir in the coconut water.
3. Pour the juice into glasses and enjoy.

PER SERVING

Calories: 37.9| Fat: 0g | Protein: 0.9g | Carbohydrates: 7.9g | Sugar: 5.9g

Carrot and Apple Juice with Ginger

Prep time: 10 minutes | Cook time: 0 minutes | Serves 1

3 carrots
1 small pumpkin, cut into cubes
1 apple (or pear)
½-inch ginger
¼ teaspoon of spices such as cinnamon, cloves or nutmeg

1. Using a sharp knife peel the pumpkin, cut into cubes. Core the apple and run through a juicer along with carrots, ginger, and pumpkin.
2. Pour into a glass, stir in the spices and drink immediately.

PER SERVING

Calories: 84.9| Fat: 0g | Protein: 0.9g | Carbohydrates: 20.9g | Sugar: 13.9g

Clementine Lemon and Carrots Juice

Prep time: 10 minutes | Cook time: 0 minutes | Serves 2

1 romaine heart
5 large carrots
½ lemon, peeled
2 clementine, peeled
1-inch knob of fresh ginger

1. Peel the lemon, clementine, and carrots and run through a juicer along with romaine heart, and ginger.
2. For better results, drink this juice once a day.

PER SERVING

Calories: 75.9| Fat: 0g | Protein: 0.9g | Carbohydrates: 17.9g | Sugar: 8.5g

Peas and Carrots with Beetroot and Celery

Prep time: 10 minutes | Cook time: 0 minutes | Serves 1

1 golden beetroot
3 large carrots
4 stalks celery
½ cucumber
½ thumb of ginger
1 medium pear

1. Thoroughly wash all ingredients and cut into pieces. Process them through a juicer.
2. Pour the juice into a glass and enjoy.

PER SERVING

Calories: 55.9| Fat: 0g | Protein: 0.9g | Carbohydrates: 11.9g | Sugar: 5.9g

Minty Pineapple and Green Juice

Prep time: 10 minutes | Cook time: 0 minutes | Serves 2

1 cup pineapple
4 large lettuce leaves
15 mint leaves
½ cup coconut water

1. Wash the lettuce and mint.
2. Trim the ends and skin from the pineapple, then remove the core and discard. Cut pineapple into 1-inch chunks.
3. Place a pitcher under the juicer's spout to collect the juice.
4. Feed the first three ingredients through the juicer's intake tube in the order listed.
5. When the juice stops flowing, remove the pitcher, add the coconut water, and stir.
6. Serve immediately.

PER SERVING

Calories: 70.9| Total Fat: 0.9g| Sugar: 13.9g| Carbohydrates: 20.9g| Fiber: 0.9g| Protein: 1.9g

Spinach Cilantro and Lettuce Juice

Prep time: 10 minutes | Cook time: 0 minutes | Serves 2

1 cup pineapple
1 cup spinach
1 cup chopped lettuce leaves
1 cucumber
10 sprigs cilantro

1. Wash all the ingredients except the pineapple.
2. Trim the ends and skin from the pineapple, then remove the core and discard. Cut pineapple into 1-inch chunks.
3. Trim the ends from the cucumber, then cut into 4-inch pieces.
4. Place a pitcher under the juicer's spout to collect the juice.
5. Feed each ingredient through the juicer's intake tube in the order listed.
6. When the juice stops flowing, remove the pitcher and stir the juice.
7. Serve immediately.

PER SERVING

Calories: 86.9| Total Fat: 0.9g| Sugar: 14.9g| Carbohydrates: 24.9g| Fiber: 0.9g| Protein: 2.9g

Orange Parsley Green Tea Juice

Prep time: 10 minutes | Cook time: 0 minutes | Serves 2

¾ cup green tea, cooled
10 dandelion greens
10 parsley sprigs
1 orange

1. Brew the green tea and let cool.
2. Wash the dandelion greens, parsley, and orange.
3. Peel the orange and separate into sections.
4. Place a pitcher under the juicer's spout to collect the juice.
5. Feed the dandelion greens, parsley, and orange through the juicer's intake tube in the order listed.
6. When the juice stops flowing, remove the pitcher, add the green tea to the juice, and stir.
7. Serve immediately.

PER SERVING

Calories: 60.9| Total Fat: 0.9g| Sugar: 8.9g| Carbohydrates: 17.9g| Fiber: 0.9g| Protein: 2.9g

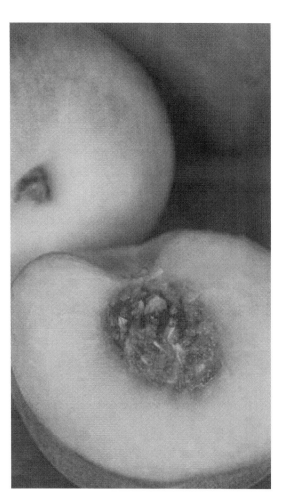

Cucumber Matcha and Lettuce Apple Juice

Prep time: 10 minutes | Cook time: 0 minutes | Serves 2

½ cup water
1 tsp matcha powder
4 green lettuce leaves
½ cucumber
½ lemon
½ green apple

1. Heat the water to 180°F. Whisk in the matcha powder and let cool.
2. Wash the lettuce, cucumber, lemon, and apple.
3. Trim the ends from the cucumber, then cut into 4-inch pieces.
4. Peel the lemon and cut into quarters.
5. Remove the apple core and discard. Cut the apple into quarters, leaving the peel intact.
6. Place a pitcher under the juicer's spout to collect the juice.
7. Feed the lettuce, cucumber, lemon, and apple through the juicer's intake tube in the order listed.
8. When the juice stops flowing, remove the pitcher, add the matcha mixture, and stir.
9. Serve immediately.

PER SERVING

Calories: 62.9| Total Fat: 0g| Sugar: 12.9g| Carbohydrates: 19.9g| Fiber: 0.9g| Protein: 0.9g

Asparagus Celery and Apple Juice
Prep time: 10 minutes | Cook time: 0 minutes | Serves 2

6 asparagus spears
1 green apple
2 celery ribs
¼ cup filtered water

1. Wash the asparagus, apple, and celery.
2. Trim ½ inch from the bottom of the asparagus, then cut stalks into 4-inch pieces.
3. Remove the apple core and discard. Cut the apple into quarters, leaving the peel intact.
4. Trim the ends from the celery, then cut into 4-inch pieces.
5. Place a pitcher under the juicer's spout to collect the juice.
6. Feed the asparagus, apple, and celery through the juicer's intake tube.
7. When the juice stops flowing, remove the pitcher, add the filtered water, and stir the juice.
8. Serve immediately.

PER SERVING

Calories: 60.9| Total Fat: 0g| Sugar: 12.9g| Carbohydrates: 18.9g| Fiber: 0.9g| Protein: 1.9g

Cucumber Orange Green Juice
Prep time: 10 minutes | Cook time: 0 minutes | Serves 2

2 cups mixed greens
1 orange
1 cucumber
½ lime
1 teaspoon maca powder

1. Wash the mixed greens, orange, cucumber, and lime.
2. Peel the orange and lime, then cut into quarters.
3. Trim the ends from the cucumber, then cut into 4-inch pieces.
4. Place a pitcher under the juicer's spout to collect the juice.
5. Feed the first four ingredients through the juicer's intake tube in the order listed.
6. When the juice stops flowing, remove the pitcher, add the maca powder, and stir the juice.
7. Serve immediately.

PER SERVING

Calories: 71.9| Total Fat: 0g| Sugar: 12.9g| Carbohydrates: 21.9g| Fiber: 0.9g| Protein: 2.9g

Ginger Spinach and Grapefruit Juice
Prep time: 10 minutes | Cook time: 0 minutes | Serves 2

2 cups spinach
½ grapefruit
4 celery ribs
½ apple
Fresh ginger root

1. Wash all the ingredients.
2. Peel the grapefruit and separate into sections.
3. Trim the ends from the celery, then cut into 4-inch pieces.
4. Remove the apple core and discard. Cut the apple into quarters, leaving the peel intact.
5. Slice off a 1-inch piece of the ginger root.
6. Place a pitcher under the juicer's spout to collect the juice.
7. Feed each ingredient through the juicer's intake tube in the order listed.
8. When the juice stops flowing, remove the pitcher and stir the juice.
9. Serve immediately.

PER SERVING

Calories: 70.9| Total Fat: 10.9| Sugar: 12.9g| Carbohydrates: 21.9g| Fiber: 0.9g| Protein: 2.9g

Chapter 7
Detoxifying and Cleansing Juices

Radish and Carrot Garlicky Detox Juice

Prep time: 5 minutes | Cook time: 0 minutes | Serves 1

2 garlic cloves
3 medium carrots
1 medium beet
1 radish
A handful of parsley

1. Peel the beet, carrots, radish, and garlic and wash the parsley.
2. Run all ingredients through a juicer and drink immediately.
3. Great to drink 1-2 times a day.

PER SERVING

Calories: 89.9| Fat: 0g | Protein: 1.1g | Carbohydrates: 20.9g | Sugar: 10.9g

Beet Cucumber and Cabbage Juice

Prep time: 5 minutes | Cook time: 0 minutes | Serves 1

½ medium cucumber
1 smallish beet
2 red or green cabbage leaves
4 medium carrots

1. Thoroughly wash the vegetables.
2. Cut the carrot ends and discard the greens.
3. Peel the beet and quarter it.
4. Pass all the ingredients through a juicer, pour into a glass and drink immediately.

PER SERVING

Calories: 55.9| Fat: 0g | Protein: 0.9g | Carbohydrates: 12.9g | Sugar: 5.5g

Veggie Boosted Detox Juice with Ginger

Prep time: 10 minutes | Cook time: 0 minutes | Serves 1

2 medium beets
3 medium tomatoes
3 long carrots, cut
Small piece of ginger

1. Wash all the vegetables and pass through a juicer.
2. Pour the juice into a glass and enjoy.

PER SERVING

Calories: 70.9| Fat: 0g | Protein: 1.1g | Carbohydrates: 15.9g | Sugar: 97.9

5 Minute Lemony Cabbage Celery Juice

Prep time: 5 minutes | Cook time: 0 minutes | Serves 1

- 1 bunch celery
- ½ head purple cabbage
- 1 lemon

1. Process the celery, purple cabbage, and lemon through a juicer.
2. Pour into a glass over ice and enjoy.

PER SERVING

Calories: 50.9| Fat: 0g | Protein: 1.1g | Carbohydrates: 11.9g | Sugar: 5.9g

Sweet Potato and Zucchini Detox Juice

Prep time: 15 minutes | Cook time: 0 minutes | Serves 1

1 cup spinach
1 cup cubed sweet potato
3 celery ribs
1 zucchini
1 cucumber
½ lemon

1. Wash all the ingredients.
2. Peel the sweet potato and cut into small cubes.
3. Trim the ends from the celery, zucchini, and cucumber, then cut into 4-inch pieces.
4. Peel the lemon half and cut into quarters.
5. Place a pitcher under the juicer's spout to collect the juice.
6. Feed each ingredient through the juicer's intake tube in the order listed.
7. When the juice stops flowing, remove the pitcher and stir the juice.
8. Serve immediately.

PER SERVING

Calories: 56.9| Fat: 1.9g | Protein: 0g | Carbohydrates: 4.9g | Sugar: 14.9g

Apple Artichoke and Celery Juice

Prep time: 20 minutes | Cook time: 0 minutes | Serves 1

1 artichoke
1 green apple
1 cup spinach
1 celery rib

1. Wash all the ingredients.
2. Prepare the artichoke per the instructions in the Preparation Tip.
3. Remove the apple core and discard. Cut the apple into quarters, leaving the peel intact.
4. Trim the ends from the celery, then cut into 4-inch pieces.
5. Place a pitcher under the juicer's spout to collect the juice. Then, feed each ingredient through the juicer's intake tube in the order listed.
6. When the juice stops flowing, remove the pitcher and stir the juice.
7. Serve immediately.

PER SERVING

Calories: 74.9| Fat: 0g | Protein: 3.9g | Carbohydrates: 24.9g | Sugar: 11.9g

Refreshing Romaine Cabbage and Pear Juice

Prep time: 5 minutes | Cook time: 0 minutes | Serves 2

1 cup red cabbage
1 firm pear
8 medium romaine leaves

1. Peel, cut, deseed, and/or chop the ingredients as needed.
2. Place a container under the juicer's spout.
3. Feed the ingredients in the order listed, through the juicer.
4. Alternate ingredients, finishing with the romaine.
5. Stir the juice and pour into glasses to serve.

PER SERVING

Calories: 32.9| Fat: 0g | Protein: 1.9g | Carbohydrates: 6.9g | Sugar: 2.9g

Cilantro Cucumber and Pear Delight

Prep time: 5 minutes | Cook time: 0 minutes | Serves 1

1 medium zucchini
1 firm pear
Handful cilantro
½ large cucumber

1. Peel, cut, deseed, and/or chop the ingredients as needed.
2. Place a container under the juicer's spout.
3. Feed the ingredients in the order listed, through the juicer.
4. Alternate ingredients, finishing with the cucumber.
5. Stir the juice and pour into glasses to serve.

PER SERVING

Calories: 50.9| Fat: 0g | Protein: 0.9g | Carbohydrates: 14.9g | Sugar: 9.9g

Kale Cabbage and Plum Cocktail

Prep time: 10 minutes | Cook time: 0 minutes | Serves 2

1 cup red cabbage
2 medium kale leaves
1 medium red apple
½ red or black plum
½ large cucumber

1. Peel, cut, deseed, and/or chop the ingredients as needed.
2. Place a container under the juicer's spout.
3. Feed the ingredients in the order listed, through the juicer.
4. Alternate ingredients, finishing with the cucumber.
5. Stir the juice and pour into glasses to serve.

PER SERVING

Calories: 79.9| Fat: 0g | Protein: 0.9g | Carbohydrates: 19.9g | Sugar: 14.9g

Pear Parsley and Carrots Cleansing Juice

Prep time: 5 minutes | Cook time: 0 minutes | Serves 2

4 large carrots
Handful parsley
1 firm pear

1. Peel, cut, deseed, and/or chop the ingredients as needed.
2. Place a container under the juicer's spout.
3. Feed the ingredients in the order listed, through the juicer.
4. Alternate ingredients, finishing with the pear.
5. Stir the juice and pour into glasses to serve.

PER SERVING

Calories: 50.9| Fat: 0g | Protein: 0.9g | Carbohydrates: 13.9g | Sugar: 6.5g

Grapes Cilantro and Zucchini Juice

Prep time: 10 minutes | Cook time: 0 minutes | Serves 2

4 large dandelion leaves
2 medium radishes
1 medium zucchini
Handful cilantro
1 cup black, purple, or red grapes
1 small orange, red, or yellow bell pepper

1. Peel, cut, deseed, and/or chop the ingredients as needed.
2. Place a container under the juicer's spout.
3. Feed the ingredients in the order listed, through the juicer.
4. Alternate ingredients, finishing with the bell pepper.
5. Stir the juice and pour into glasses to serve.

PER SERVING

Calories: 32.9| Fat: 0.9g | Protein: 9.9g | Carbohydrates: 20.9g | Sugar: 1.9g

Carrots and Turmeric Root Juice

Prep time: 10 minutes | Cook time: 0 minutes | Serves 2

4 medium carrots
1-inch piece fresh turmeric root
Handful parsley
1 large orange, red, or yellow bell pepper
Freshly ground black pepper(optional)

1. Peel, cut, deseed, and/or chop the ingredients as needed.
2. Place a container under the juicer's spout.
3. Feed the ingredients in the order listed, through the juicer.
4. Alternate the produce, finishing with the bell pepper.
5. Stir the black pepper (if using) directly into the juice to increase your absorption of the curcumin in the turmeric.

PER SERVING

Calories: 49.9| Fat: 0g | Protein: 0.9g | Carbohydrates: 10.9g | Sugar: 5.9g

Lemony Spinach and Cilantro Detox Juice

Prep time: 10 minutes | Cook time: 0 minutes | Serves 2

1 large orange, red, or yellow bell pepper
2 large carrots
Handful spinach
1 small lemon
1-inch piece fresh turmeric root
Handful cilantro
½ large cucumber
Freshly ground black pepper(optional)

1. Peel, cut, deseed, and/or chop the ingredients as needed.
2. Place a container under the juicer's spout.
3. Feed the ingredients in the order listed, through the juicer.
4. Alternate the produce, finishing with the cucumber.
5. Stir the black pepper (if using) directly into the juice to increase your absorption of the curcumin in the turmeric.

PER SERVING

Calories: 95.9| Fat: 1.9g | Protein: 1.9g | Carbohydrates: 21.9g | Sugar: 9.9g

Parsley Celery and Cauliflower Juice

Prep time: 10 minutes | Cook time: 0 minutes | Serves 2

1 cup cauliflower
1 firm pear
8 parsley sprigs
4 large celery stalks

1. Peel, cut, deseed, and/or chop the ingredients as needed.
2. Place a container under the juicer's spout.
3. Feed the ingredients in the order listed, through the juicer.
4. Alternate ingredients, finishing with the celery.
5. Stir the juice and pour into glasses to serve.

PER SERVING

Calories: 19.9| Fat: 0g | Protein: 0.9g | Carbohydrates: 3.9g | Sugar: 1.9g

Collard Kale and Cucumber Juice

Prep time: 15 minutes | Cook time: 0 minutes | Serves 2

1 red bell pepper
2 large carrots
1 small collard leaf
1 medium kale leaf
½ large cucumber
Handful cilantro or parsley
1 medium red apple

1. Peel, cut, deseed, and/or chop the ingredients as needed.
2. Place a container under the juicer's spout.
3. Feed the ingredients in the order listed, through the juicer.
4. Alternate ingredients, finishing with the apple.
5. Stir the juice and pour into glasses to serve.

PER SERVING

Calories: 93.9| Fat: 0g | Protein: 1.9g | Carbohydrates: 22.9g | Sugar: 14.9g

10 Minute Cabbage Spinach and Pineapple

Prep time: 10 minutes | Cook time: 0 minutes | Serves 2

1 cup red cabbage
Handful spinach
1 cup pineapple
2 Cara or other small oranges, peeled

1. Peel, cut, deseed, and/or chop the ingredients as needed.
2. Place a container under the juicer's spout.
3. Feed the ingredients in the order listed, through the juicer.
4. Alternate ingredients, finishing with the orange or the pineapple.
5. Stir the juice and pour into glasses to serve.

PER SERVING

Calories: 87.9| Fat: 0.9g | Protein: 22.9g | Carbohydrates: 19.9g | Sugar: 19.9g

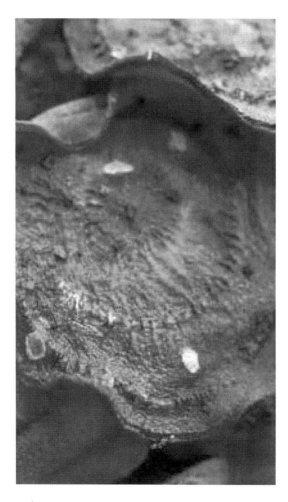

Zucchini Kale and Radishes with Broccoli

Prep time: 15 minutes | Cook time: 0 minutes | Serves 3

4-inch piece broccoli stem
4 large kale leaves
2 medium radishes
1 medium zucchini
1 firm pear
1 medium apple
1 cup fresh coconut water

1. Peel, cut, deseed, and/or chop the ingredients as needed.
2. Place a container under the juicer's spout.
3. Feed the ingredients in the order listed, through the juicer.
4. Alternate the produce, finishing with the apple.
5. Stir the coconut water directly into the juice.

PER SERVING

Calories: 71.9| Fat: 0g | Protein: 0.9g | Carbohydrates: 16.9g | Sugar: 12.9g

Swiss Chard with Broccoli and Apple Juice

Prep time: 10 minutes | Cook time: 0 minutes | Serves 2

4-inch piece broccoli stem
4 large Swiss chard leaves
1 medium apple
2 large celery stalks

1. Peel, cut, deseed, and/or chop the ingredients as needed.
2. Place a container under the juicer's spout.
3. Feed the ingredients in the order listed, through the juicer.
4. Alternate the produce, finishing with the celery or the apple.
5. Stir the juice and pour into glasses to serve.

PER SERVING

Calories: 50.9| Fat: 0g | Protein: 0g | Carbohydrates: 12.9g | Sugar: 9.9g

Kale Watermelon and Carrot Juice

Prep time: 10 minutes | Cook time: 0 minutes | Serves 2

2 large carrots
2 large kale leaves
½ red apple
1 cup watermelon

1. Peel, cut, deseed, and/or chop the ingredients as needed.
2. Place a container under the juicer's spout.
3. Feed the ingredients in the order listed, through the juicer.
4. Alternate ingredients, finishing with the watermelon.
5. Stir the juice and pour into glasses to serve

PER SERVING

Calories: 83.9| Fat: 0g | Protein: 0.9g | Carbohydrates: 19.9g | Sugar: 13.9g

Refreshing Kiwi Plus Bok Choy Drink

Prep time: 10 minutes | Cook time: 0 minutes | Serves 2

2 large Bok choy stems
2 kiwifruits
1 cup watermelon

1. Peel, cut, deseed, and/or chop the ingredients as needed.
2. Place a container under the juicer's spout.
3. Feed the ingredients in the order listed, through the juicer.
4. Alternate ingredients, finishing with the watermelon or the pineapple.
5. Stir the juice and pour into glasses to serve

PER SERVING

Calories: 27.9| Fat: 0.9g | Protein: 0.9g | Carbohydrates: 0.9g | Sugar: 4.9g

Potato Carrot and Kale Detox Juice

Prep time: 10 minutes | Cook time: 0 minutes | Serves 3

4 extra-large carrots
2 large kale leaves
1 small, sweet potato, peeled

1. Peel, cut, deseed, and/or chop the ingredients as needed.
2. Place a container under the juicer's spout.
3. Feed the ingredients in the order listed, through the juicer.
4. Alternate ingredients, finishing with the sweet potato.
5. Stir the juice and pour into glasses to serve

PER SERVING

Calories: 26.9| Fat: 0.9g | Protein: 0.9g | Carbohydrates: 8.9g | Sugar: 1.9g

Tangy Sweet Potato with Spinach

Prep time: 15 minutes | Cook time: 0 minutes | Serves 2

3 cups spinach
½ small, sweet potato, peeled
8 parsley sprigs
½ medium lemon
4 large celery stalks

1. Peel, cut, deseed, and/or chop the ingredients as needed.
2. Place a container under the juicer's spout.
3. Feed the ingredients in the order listed, through the juicer.
4. Alternate ingredients, finishing with celery.
5. Stir the juice and pour into glasses to serve.

PER SERVING

Calories: 19.9| Fat: 0g | Protein: 1.9g | Carbohydrates: 3.9g | Sugar: 0.9g

Orange Potato and Turmeric Roots Refresher

Prep time: 10 minutes | Cook time: 0 minutes | Serves 2

4 large carrots
1-inch piece fresh turmeric root
1 small, sweet potato, peeled
Freshly ground black pepper(optional)

1. Peel, cut, deseed, and/or chop the ingredients as needed.
2. Place a container under the juicer's spout.
3. Feed the ingredients in the order listed, through the juicer.
4. Alternate the produce, finishing with the sweet potato.
5. Stir the black pepper (if using) directly into the juice to increase your absorption of the curcumin in the turmeric.

PER SERVING

Calories: 85.9| Fat: 0g | Protein: 1.9g | Carbohydrates: 19.9g | Sugar: 97.9

Gingered Apple Cucumber Detox Juice

Prep time: 5 minutes | Cook time: 0 minutes | Serves 1

1 medium golden or red beet
1-inch piece fresh ginger root
1-inch piece fresh turmeric root
12 parsley sprigs
1 medium red apple
1 large cucumber
Freshly ground black pepper(optional)

1. Peel, cut, deseed, and/or chop the ingredients as needed.
2. Place a container under the juicer's spout.
3. Feed the ingredients in the order listed, through the juicer.
4. Alternate the produce, finishing with the cucumber.
5. Stir the black pepper (if using) directly into the juice to increase your absorption of the curcumin in the turmeric.

PER SERVING

Calories: 83.9| Fat: 0g | Protein: 1.9g | Carbohydrates: 19.9g | Sugar: 13.9g

Celery Cucumber and Orange Spinach Cleanser

Prep time: 10 minutes | Cook time: 0 minutes | Serves 2

3 large carrots
2 large celery stalks
Handful spinach
8 parsley sprigs
2 medium oranges, peeled
½ large cucumber

1. Peel, cut, deseed, and/or chop the ingredients as needed.
2. Place a container under the juicer's spout.
3. Feed the ingredients in the order listed, through the juicer.
4. Alternate ingredients, finishing with the cucumber.
5. Stir the juice and pour into glasses to serve.

PER SERVING

Calories: 56.9| Fat: 0g | Protein: 1.9g | Carbohydrates: 12.9g | Sugar: 5.9g

Tangy Kale plus Bok Choy Drink

Prep time: 10 minutes | Cook time: 0 minutes | Serves 2

1 small baby Bok choy
3 large kale leaves
1 medium apple
1 small lemon
½-inch piece gingerroot

1. Peel, cut, deseed, and/or chop the ingredients as needed.
2. Place a container under the juicer's spout.
3. Feed the ingredients one at a time, in the order listed, through the juicer.
4. Stir the juice and pour into glasses to serve.

PER SERVING

Calories: 52.9| Fat: 0g | Protein: 0g | Carbohydrates: 13.9g | Sugar: 9.9g

Chapter 8
Anti-Aging and Energizing Juices

Carrot Apple and Celery Energizing Juice

Prep time: 5 minutes | Cook time: 0 minutes | Serves 2

1 bunch parsley leaves
2 medium carrots
2 large stalks celery
1 small apple

1. Peel, cut, deseed, and/or chop the ingredients as needed.
2. Place a container under the juicer's spout.
3. Feed the ingredients one at a time, in the order listed, through the juicer.
4. Stir the juice and pour into glasses to serve.

PER SERVING

Calories: 76.9| Fat: 0.9g | Protein: 1.9g | Carbohydrates: 18.9g | Sugar: 10.9g

Power Collards Broccoli and Kale Juice

Prep time: 5 minutes | Cook time: 0 minutes | Serves 2

1 bunch kale leaves
1 small head broccoli
1 large stalk celery
½ bunch collard greens
1 tablespoon hempseed

1. 1. Peel, cut, deseed, and/or chop the ingredients as needed.
2. 2. Place a container under the juicer's spout.
3. 3. Feed the first four ingredients one at a time, in the order listed, through the juicer.
4. 4. Stir the hempseed into the juice and pour into glasses to serve.

PER SERVING

Calories: 24.9| Fat: 0.9g | Protein: 2.9g | Carbohydrates: 3.9g | Sugar: 0.9g

Kale Celery Berry Juice with Cucumber

Prep time: 5 minutes | Cook time: 0 minutes | Serves 1

6 strawberries
6 kale leaves
2 celery ribs
½ cucumber

1. Wash all the ingredients.
2. Trim the ends from the celery and cucumber, then cut into 4-inch pieces.
3. Place a pitcher under the juicer's spout to collect the juice.
4. Feed each ingredient through the juicer's intake tube in the order listed.
5. When the juice stops flowing, remove the pitcher and stir the juice.
6. Serve immediately.

PER SERVING

Calories: 83.9| Fat: 1.9g | Protein: 7.9g | Carbohydrates: 21.9g | Sugar: 7.9mg

Anti-Aging Spinach and Artichoke Juice

Prep time: 5 minutes | Cook time: 0 minutes | Serves 1

1 artichoke
1 green apple
1 cup spinach
1 celery rib

1. Wash all the ingredients.
2. Prepare the artichoke per the instructions in the Preparation Tip.
3. Remove the apple core and discard. Cut the apple into quarters, leaving the peel intact.
4. Trim the ends from the celery, then cut into 4-inch pieces.
5. Place a pitcher under the juicer's spout to collect the juice. Then, feed each ingredient through the juicer's intake tube in the order listed.
6. When the juice stops flowing, remove the pitcher and stir the juice.
7. Serve immediately.

PER SERVING

Calories: 74.9| Fat: 0g | Protein: 3.9g | Carbohydrates: 24.9g | Sugar: 11.9mg

Collard Leaves and Blackberry Power Juice

Prep time: 5 minutes | Cook time: 0 minutes | Serves 1

½ cup blackberries
4 large collard green leaves
½ lime
8 ounces sparkling mineral water

1. Wash the blackberries, collard greens, and lime.
2. Peel the lime and cut into quarters.
3. Feed the first three ingredients through the juicer's intake tube in the order listed.
4. When the juice stops flowing, remove the pitcher, add the mineral water, and stir the juice.
5. Serve immediately.

PER SERVING

Calories: 29.9| Fat: 0.9g | Protein: 2.9g | Carbohydrates: 11.9g | Sugar: 2.9mg

5 Minute Spinach Berry and Coconut Juice

Prep time: 5 minutes | Cook time: 0 minutes | Serves 1

2 cups spinach
6 celery ribs
1 cup blueberries
8 ounces coconut water

1. Wash the spinach, celery, and blueberries.
2. Trim the ends from the celery, then cut into 4-inch pieces.
3. Place a pitcher under the juicer's spout to collect the juice.
4. Feed the first three ingredients through the juicer's intake tube in the order listed.
5. When the juice stops flowing, remove the pitcher, add the coconut water, and stir.
6. Serve immediately.

PER SERVING

Calories: 72.9| Fat: 0.9g | Protein: 2.9g | Carbohydrates: 20.9g | Sugar: 12.9mg

Apple Berry Green Tea Juice with Spinach

Prep time: 5 minutes | Cook time: 0 minutes | Serves 1

¾ cup green tea
2 cups spinach
1 red apple
2 teaspoons ground flax seed

1. Brew the green tea and let it cool.
2. Wash the spinach and apple.
3. Remove the apple core and discard. Cut the apple into quarters, leaving the peel intact.
4. Place a pitcher under the juicer's spout to collect the juice.
5. Feed the spinach, then the apple through the juicer's intake tube.
6. When the juice stops flowing, remove the pitcher, add the green tea and flax seed, then stir.
7. Serve immediately.

PER SERVING

Calories: 65.9| Fat: 1.9g | Protein: 1.9g | Carbohydrates: 16.9g | Sugar: 10.9mg

Minty Cucumbers and Gingered Carrot Juice

Prep time: 5 minutes | Cook time: 0 minutes | Serves 1

2 cucumbers
3 carrots
2 tablespoons parsley
1 sprig mint leaves
Fresh ginger root

1. Wash all the ingredients.
2. Trim the ends from the cucumbers and carrots, then cut into 4-inch pieces.
3. Slice off a ½-inch piece of the ginger root.
4. Place a pitcher under the juicer's spout to collect the juice.
5. Feed each ingredient through the juicer's intake tube in the order listed.
6. When the juice stops flowing, remove the pitcher and stir the juice.
7. Serve immediately.

PER SERVING

Calories: 93.9| Fat: 0.9g | Protein: 3.9g | Carbohydrates: 25.9g | Sugar: 10.9mg

5 Minute Cucumber Celery Limey Juice

Prep time: 5 minutes | Cook time: 0 minutes | Serves 1

1 cucumber
1 romaine heart
4 celery ribs
1 lime
½ tablespoon wheatgrass powder

1. Wash the cucumber, romaine, celery, and lime.
2. Trim the ends from the cucumber and celery, then cut into 4-inch pieces.
3. Peel the lime and cut into quarters.
4. Place a pitcher under the juicer's spout to collect the juice.
5. Feed the first four ingredients through the juicer's intake tube in the order listed.
6. When the juice stops flowing, remove the pitcher, add the wheatgrass powder, and stir the juice.
7. Serve immediately.

PER SERVING

Calories: 97.9| Fat: 0.9g | Protein: 6.9g | Carbohydrates: 25.9g | Sugar: 7.9mg

Tangy Chad with Beet Cucumber Juice

Prep time: 5 minutes | Cook time: 0 minutes | Serves 1

1 cucumber
1 Swiss chard leaf
2 sprigs cilantro
½ small to medium size beet
3 celery ribs
½ lemon
Fresh ginger root

1. Wash all the ingredients.
2. Trim the ends from the cucumber and celery, then cut into 4-inch pieces.
3. Remove any greens from the beet and save for juicing later. Cut the beet into quarters.
4. Peel the lemon and cut into quarters.
5. Slice off a 1-inch piece of the ginger root.
6. Place a pitcher under the juicer's spout to collect the juice.
7. Feed each ingredient through the juicer's intake tube in the order listed.
8. When the juice stops flowing, remove the pitcher and stir the juice.
9. Serve immediately.

PER SERVING

Calories: 75.9| Fat: 0.9g | Protein: 3.9g | Carbohydrates: 21.9g | Sugar: 9.9mg

Cinnamon Berry and Gingered Spinach Juice

Prep time: 5 minutes | Cook time: 0 minutes | Serves 1

1 cup blueberries
2 cups spinach
1 cucumber
Fresh ginger root
½ teaspoon maca powder
¼ teaspoon cinnamon

1. Wash the blueberries, spinach, cucumber, and ginger root.
2. Trim the ends from the cucumber, then cut into 4-inch pieces.
3. Slice off a ½-inch piece of the ginger root.
4. Place a pitcher under the juicer's spout to collect the juice.
5. Feed the first four ingredients through the juicer's intake tube in the order listed.
6. When the juice stops flowing, remove the pitcher, add the maca powder and cinnamon, then stir.
7. Serve immediately.

PER SERVING

Calories: 94.9| Fat: 0.9g | Protein: 3.9g | Carbohydrates: 26.9g | Sugar: 13.9mg

Watermelon Zucchini and Limey Coconut Water

Prep time: 5 minutes | Cook time: 0 minutes | Serves 2

1 medium zucchini
1 lime, peeled
1 cup watermelon
½ cup fresh coconut water

1. Peel, cut, deseed, and/or chop the ingredients as needed.
2. Place a container under the juicer's spout.
3. Alternate the produce, finishing with the watermelon. Stir the coconut water directly into the juice.
4. Pour into glasses to serve.

PER SERVING

Calories: 81.9| Fat: 0.9g | Protein: 1.9g | Carbohydrates: 19.9g | Sugar: 12.9g

Lemony Kale and Cucumber Beet Juice

Prep time: 10 minutes | Cook time: 0 minutes | Serves 3

1 medium golden or red beet
2 large kale leaves
5 parsley sprigs
1 apple
½ lemon
1 large cucumber

1. Peel, cut, deseed, and/or chop the ingredients as needed.
2. Place a container under the juicer's spout.
3. Alternate ingredients, finishing with the cucumber.
4. Stir the juice and pour into glasses to serve.

PER SERVING

Calories: 84.9| Fat: 0g | Protein: 0.9g | Carbohydrates: 20.9g | Sugar: 13.9g

10 Minute Kale Berry Green Juice

Prep time: 10 minutes | Cook time: 0 minutes | Serves 2

6 strawberries
6 kale leaves
2 celery ribs
½ cucumber

1. Wash all the ingredients.
2. Trim the ends from the celery and cucumber, then cut into 4-inch pieces.
3. Place a pitcher under the juicer's spout to collect the juice.
4. Feed each ingredient through the juicer's intake tube in the order listed.
5. When the juice stops flowing, remove the pitcher and stir the juice.
6. Serve immediately.

PER SERVING

Calories: 83.9| Total Fat: 1.9g| Sugar: 7.9g| Carbohydrates: 21.9g| Fiber: 0.9g| Protein: 7.9g

Artichoke Celery and Spinach Juice

Prep time: 10 minutes | Cook time: 0 minutes | Serves 2

1 artichoke
1 green apple
1 cup spinach
1 celery rib
1.Wash all the ingredients.

1. Prepare the artichoke per the instructions in the Preparation Tip.
2. Remove the apple core and discard. Cut the apple into quarters, leaving the peel intact.
3. Trim the ends from the celery, then cut into 4-inch pieces.
4. Place a pitcher under the juicer's spout to collect the juice. Then, feed each ingredient through the juicer's intake tube in the order listed.
5. When the juice stops flowing, remove the pitcher and stir the juice.
6. Serve immediately.
7. Slice the stem from the artichoke and cut it into small pieces.
8. Trim 1 to 2 inches off the top.
9. Press down on the center to open the leaves.
10. Rinse well under running water.
11. Scoop out the hairy center with a grapefruit spoon.
12. Tear or cut away the leaves.
13. Place into a food processor or blender and process until the consistency is even.

PER SERVING

Calories: 74.9| Total Fat: 0g| Sugar: 11.9g| Carbohydrates: 24.9g| Fiber: 0.9g| Protein: 3.9g

Blackberry Collard Limey Green Juice

Prep time: 10 minutes | Cook time: 0 minutes | Serves 2

½ cup blackberries
4 large collard green leaves
½ lime
8 ounces sparkling mineral water

1. Wash the blackberries, collard greens, and lime.
2. Peel the lime and cut into quarters.
3. Feed the first three ingredients through the juicer's intake tube in the order listed.
4. When the juice stops flowing, remove the pitcher, add the mineral water, and stir the juice.
5. Serve immediately.

PER SERVING

Calories: 29.9| Total Fat: 0.9g| Sugar: 2.9g| Carbohydrates: 11.9g| Fiber: 0.9g| Protein: 2.9g

Lettuce and Carrots Salad Juice

Prep time: 10 minutes | Cook time: 0 minutes | Serves 2

3 carrots
6 romaine lettuce leaves
2 medium tomatoes
2 green onions
½ green bell pepper
¼ cup parsley
½ lemon

1. Wash all the ingredients.
2. Trim the ends from carrots and green onions, then cut into 4-inch pieces.
3. Remove the stems from the tomatoes and cut into quarters.
4. Remove the stem and seeds from the bell pepper. Cut into small pieces.
5. Peel the lemon half and cut into quarters.
6. Place a pitcher under the juicer's spout to collect the juice.
7. Feed each ingredient through the juicer's intake tube in the order listed.
8. When the juice stops flowing, remove the pitcher and stir the juice.
9. Serve immediately.

PER SERVING

Calories: 88.9| Total Fat: 0.9g| Sugar: 13.9g| Carbohydrates: 27.9g| Fiber: 0.9g| Protein: 4.9g

10 Minute Veggies plus Sprouts Drink

Prep time: 10 minutes | Cook time: 0 minutes | Serves 2

4 celery ribs
1 cucumber
8 lettuce leaves
½ cup alfalfa sprouts

1. Wash all the ingredients.
2. Trim the ends from the celery and cucumber, then cut into 4-inch pieces.
3. Place a pitcher under the juicer's spout to collect the juice.
4. Feed each ingredient through the juicer's intake tube in the order listed.
5. When the juice stops flowing, remove the pitcher and stir the juice.
6. Serve immediately.

PER SERVING

Calories: 54.9| Total Fat: 0.9g| Sugar: 6.9g| Carbohydrates: 15.9g| Fiber: 0.9g| Protein: 4.9g

Limey Kale and Watermelon Juice

Prep time: 10 minutes | Cook time: 0 minutes | Serves 2

1½ cups watermelon
4 kale leaves
½ lime
2 celery ribs

1. Wash the kale, lime, and celery.
2. Cut the watermelon into quarters. Remove the rind and discard. Cut the watermelon into smaller pieces.
3. Trim the ends from the celery, then cut into 4-inch pieces.
4. Peel the lime half and cut into quarters.
5. Place a pitcher under the juicer's spout to collect the juice.
6. Feed each ingredient through the juicer's intake tube in the order listed.
7. When the juice stops flowing, remove the pitcher and stir the juice.
8. Serve immediately.

PER SERVING

Calories: 89.9| Total Fat: 0.9g| Sugar: 12.9g| Carbohydrates: 23.9g| Fiber: 0.9g| Protein: 5.9g

Honeydew and Cabbage Lemonade

Prep time: 10 minutes | Cook time: 0 minutes | Serves 2

1 cup honeydew melon
4 collard green leaves
3 cups cabbage
1 lemon

1. Wash the collard greens, cabbage, and lemon.
2. Cut the honeydew melon into quarters. Remove the rind and discard. Cut the melon into small pieces.
3. Cut the cabbage in half, then slice or chop into smaller pieces.
4. Peel the lemon and cut into quarters.
5. Place a pitcher under the juicer's spout to collect the juice.
6. Feed each ingredient through the juicer's intake tube in the order listed.
7. When the juice stops flowing, remove the pitcher and stir the juice.
8. Serve immediately.

PER SERVING

Calories: 84.9| Total Fat: 0.9g| Sugar: 15.9g| Carbohydrates: 28.9g| Fiber: 0.9g| Protein: 4.9g

10 Minute Apple Cucumber Alkalizing Juice

Prep time: 10 minutes | Cook time: 0 minutes | Serves 2

3 cups spinach
1 red apple
½ cucumber
¼ cup filtered water
½ tablespoon wheatgrass powder
1 tablespoon apple cider vinegar

1. Wash the spinach, apple, and cucumber.
2. Remove the apple core and discard. Cut the apple into quarters, leaving the peel intact.
3. Trim the ends from the cucumber, then cut into 4-inch pieces.
4. Place a pitcher under the juicer's spout to collect the juice.
5. Feed the first three ingredients through the juicer's intake tube in the order listed.
6. When the juice stops flowing, remove the pitcher, add the water, wheatgrass powder and apple cider vinegar, and stir the juice.
7. Serve immediately.

PER SERVING

Calories: 97.9| Total Fat: 0.9g| Sugar: 12.9g| Carbohydrates: 21.9g| Fiber: 1.9g| Protein: 57.9

Plum Tomato Cucumber and Peppered Gazpacho

Prep time: 5 minutes | Cook time: 0 minutes | Serves 1

8 plum tomatoes
2 large cucumbers
4 celery sticks
2 sweet red (bell) peppers
¼ small red onion
3 large handfuls of parsley
2 limes (optional)
sea salt and freshly ground pepper

1. Peel, cut, deseed, and/or chop the ingredients as needed.
2. Place a container under the juicer's spout.
3. Feed the ingredients one at a time, in the order listed, through the juicer.
4. Stir the juice and pour into glasses to serve.

PER SERVING

Calories: 111| Fat: 0g | Protein: 20g | Carbohydrates: 1g | Sugar: 89mg

Celery Chard and Basil Refreshing Juice

Prep time: 10 minutes | Cook time: 0 minutes | Serves 2

Handful spinach
2 large Swiss chard leaves
1 cup blueberries
½ lemon
8 large basil leaves
2 large celery stalks

1. Peel, cut, deseed, and/or chop the ingredients as needed.
2. Place a container under the juicer's spout.
3. Feed the ingredients one at a time, in the order listed, through the juicer.
4. Stir the juice and pour into glasses to serve.

PER SERVING

Calories: 117.9| Fat: 0g | Protein: 0.9g | Carbohydrates: 29.9g | Sugar: 37.9mg

Romaine Cucumber and Pepper Juice

Prep time: 5 minutes | Cook time: 0 minutes | Serves 2

1 orange, red, or yellow bell pepper
4 romaine leaves
2 small oranges, peeled
1 large cucumber
Alternate ingredients, finishing with the cucumber.

1. Peel, cut, deseed, and/or chop the ingredients as needed.
2. Place a container under the juicer's spout.
3. Feed the ingredients one at a time, in the order listed, through the juicer.
4. Stir the juice and pour into glasses to serve.

PER SERVING

Calories: 105.9| Fat: 0g | Protein: 2.9g | Carbohydrates: 23.9g | Sugar: 15.9mg

5 Minute Berry Loaded Refreshing Juice

Prep time: 5 minutes | Cook time: 0 minutes | Serves 2

3 apples, cored
1 cup of cranberry juice
1 cup of fresh blueberries

1. Process the apples and blueberries through a juicer and pour into a pitcher.
2. Add the cranberry juice, stir well, and enjoy over ice.

PER SERVING

Calories: 119.9| Fat: 0g | Protein: 0g | Carbohydrates: 29.9g | Sugar: 14.9mg

Pear Parsley and Orange Juice

Prep time: 5 minutes | Cook time: 0 minutes | Serves 2

1 medium navel orange
1 medium apple
1 medium pear
½ bunch parsley
½ lime

1. Peel, cut, deseed, and/or chop the ingredients as needed.
2. Place a container under the juicer's spout.
3. Feed the ingredients one at a time, in the order listed, through the juicer.
4. Stir the juice and pour into glasses to serve.

PER SERVING

Calories: 99| Fat: 0g | Protein: 0.9g | Carbohydrates: 26.9g | Sugar: 1.9mg

Limey Orange and Kiwi Juice

Prep time: 5 minutes | Cook time: 0 minutes | Serves 2

3 medium navel oranges
3 ripe kiwis
1 teaspoon lime zest

1. 1. Peel, cut, deseed, and/or chop the ingredients as needed.
2. 2. Place a container under the juicer's spout.
3. 3. Feed the oranges and kiwis through the juicer.
4. 4. Stir the lime zest into the juice and pour into glasses to serve.

PER SERVING

Calories: 103| Fat: 0g | Protein: 0.9g | Carbohydrates: 26.9g | Sugar: 1.9mg

Carrot Cabbage Chard and Lemony Apple

Prep time: 5 minutes | Cook time: 0 minutes | Serves 4

4 large Swiss chard leaves
2 large carrots
1 medium apple
¼ small head red cabbage
2 tablespoons freshly squeezed lemon juice

1. Peel, cut, deseed, and/or chop the ingredients as needed.
2. Place a container under the juicer's spout.
3. Feed the Swiss chard, carrots, apple, and cabbage through the juicer.
4. Stir the lemon juice into the juice and pour into glasses to serve.

PER SERVING

Calories: 101| Fat: 24.9g | Protein: 0g | Carbohydrates: 1.9g | Sugar: 15.9mg

Apple and Carrot Limeade with Mint

Prep time: 5 minutes | Cook time: 0 minutes | Serves 2

8 carrots
2 cucumbers
4 apples
1 lime
large handful of fresh mint
2-inch (5 cm) piece of fresh root ginger

1. Peel, cut, deseed, and/or chop the ingredients as needed.
2. Place a container under the juicer's spout.
3. Feed the first four ingredients one at a time, in the order listed, through the juicer.
4. Stir the juice and pour into glasses to serve.

PER SERVING

Calories: 103| Fat: 0g | Protein: 1.9g | Carbohydrates: 26.9g | Sugar: 1.9mg

Apple Carrot and Gingery Spinach Juice

Prep time: 5 minutes | Cook time: 0 minutes | Serves 1

2 stalks celery
2 small apples
2 carrots
5 small radishes
1 small piece ginger
1 cup spinach

1. Wash the apples, carrots, radishes, spinach and cut into chunks.
2. Add to a juicer along with a piece of ginger.
3. Pour the extracted juice into a glass, stir well and drink.

PER SERVING

Calories: 108| Fat: 26.9g | Protein: 0g | Carbohydrates: 0.9g | Sugar: 18.9mg

Kale Pineapple and Ginger Juice

Prep time: 5 minutes | Cook time: 0 minutes | Serves 2

1 lime
4 kale leaves
1/3 pineapple
2 red apples
1-inch knob of ginger
A handful Italian parsley

1. Wash the kale, parsley, lime, and apples. Remove the zest of the lime. Cut the apples into chunks and run through a juicer, alternating with the remaining ingredients.
2. Apples will ease the process by pushing down the other ingredients.
3. Pour the fresh juice into a tall glass and drink immediately.

PER SERVING

Calories: 99| Fat: 0g | Protein: 0.9g | Carbohydrates: 26.9g | Sugar: 18.9mg

Peppered Cabbage and Cucumber Juice

Prep time: 5 minutes | Cook time: 0 minutes | Serves 1

2 medium tomatoes
1 cucumber
1 cup spinach
1 cup cabbage
½ red bell pepper
2 celery ribs
2 carrots
1 green onion

1. Wash all the ingredients.
2. Remove stems from the tomatoes and cut into quarters.
3. Trim the ends from the cucumber, celery, carrots, and green onion, then cut into 4-inch pieces.
4. Cut cabbage in half, then slice or chop into smaller pieces.
5. Remove the stem and seeds from the bell pepper. Cut into small pieces.
6. Place a pitcher under the juicer's spout to collect the juice.
7. Feed each ingredient through the juicer's intake tube in the order listed.
8. When the juice stops flowing, remove the pitcher and stir the juice.
9. Serve immediately.

PER SERVING

Calories: 103| Fat: 0.9g | Protein: 5.9g | Carbohydrates: 29.9g | Sugar: 15.9mg

Lemony Green Beans and Spinach Juice

Prep time: 10 minutes | Cook time: 0 minutes | Serves 1

1 cup spinach
2 cups green beans
1 cucumber
½ pear
½ lemon

1. Wash all the ingredients.
2. Trim the ends from the green beans and cucumber, then cut into 4-inch pieces.
3. Cut the pear into quarters, removing the core and seeds, but leaving the peel intact.
4. Peel the lemon half and cut into quarters.
5. Place a pitcher under the juicer's spout to collect the juice.
6. Feed each ingredient through the juicer's intake tube in the order listed.
7. When the juice stops flowing, remove the pitcher and stir the juice.
8. Serve immediately.

PER SERVING

Calories: 101| Fat: 0.9g | Protein: 5.9g | Carbohydrates: 33.9g | Sugar: 15.9mg

Cacao Powder Kale Raspberry Juice

Prep time: 15 minutes | Cook time: 0 minutes | Serves 1

½ cup raspberries
4 kale leaves
½ red apple
1 cup coconut water
1 tablespoon raw cacao powder

1. Wash the raspberries, kale, and apple.
2. Remove the apple core and discard. Cut the apple into quarters, leaving the peel intact.
3. Place a pitcher under the juicer's spout to collect the juice.
4. Feed the raspberries, kale, and apple through the juicer's intake tube in the order listed.
5. When the juice stops flowing, remove the pitcher, add the coconut water and raw cacao powder, and stir the juice.
6. Serve immediately.

PER SERVING

Calories: 103.9| Fat: 1.9g | Protein: 5.9g | Carbohydrates: 26.9g | Sugar: 13.9g

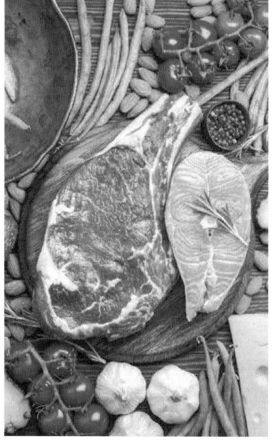

Zucchini Blended with Bok Choy

Prep time: 10 minutes | Cook time: 0 minutes | Serves 2

1 medium zucchini
2 cups black, purple, or red grapes
4 small Bok choy stems

1. Peel, cut, deseed, and/or chop the ingredients as needed.
2. Place a container under the juicer's spout.
3. Feed the ingredients in the order listed, through the juicer.
4. Alternate ingredients, finishing with the Bok choy.
5. Stir the juice and pour into glasses to serve.

PER SERVING

Calories: 104| Fat: 0g | Protein: 0.9g | Carbohydrates: 22.9g | Sugar: 22.9g

Apple Cinnamon Anti-Inflammatory Juice

Prep time: 10 minutes | Cook time: 0 minutes | Serves 1

1 cup spinach
4 carrots
2 celery ribs
1 green apple
½ teaspoon ground cinnamon

1. Wash the spinach, carrots, celery, and apple.
2. Trim the ends from the carrots and celery, then cut into 4-inch pieces.
3. Remove the apple core and discard. Cut the apple into quarters, leaving the peel intact.
4. Place a pitcher under the juicer's spout to collect the juice.
5. Feed the first four ingredients through the juicer's intake tube in the order listed.
6. When the juice stops flowing, remove the pitcher, add the cinnamon, and stir the juice.
7. Serve immediately.

PER SERVING

Calories: 105| Fat: 0.9g | Protein: 2.9g | Carbohydrates: 32.9g | Sugar: 19.9g

Dragon Fruit plus Spinach Juice

Prep time: 10 minutes | Cook time: 0 minutes | Serves 2

1 dragon fruit (pitaya)
1 small collard leaf
1 large cucumber
Handful spinach
1 small apple

1. Cut open the dragon fruit, scoop out the pulp and seeds, and discard the rind.
2. Alternate ingredients, finishing with the apple.

PER SERVING

Calories: 99| Fat: 0.9g | Protein: 1.9g | Carbohydrates: 24.9g | Sugar: 18.9g

Kiwi Pear and Cucumber Healthy Juice

Prep time: 10 minutes | Cook time: 0 minutes | Serves 2

2 kiwifruits
2 firm pears
½ large cucumber

1. Peel, cut, deseed, and/or chop the ingredients as needed.
2. **Place a container under the juicer's spout.**
3. **Feed the ingredients one at a time, in the order listed, through the juicer.**
4. **Stir the juice and pour into glasses to serve.**

PER SERVING

Calories: 101| Fat: 0.9g | Protein: 1.9g | Carbohydrates: 24.9g | Sugar: 15.9g

Pepper and Cucumber with Grapefruit Juice

Prep time: 5 minutes | Cook time: 0 minutes | Serves 2

½ large yellow bell pepper
1 pink or red grapefruit, peeled
2 cups strawberries
½ large cucumber

1. Peel, cut, deseed, and/or chop the ingredients as needed.
2. Place a container under the juicer's spout.
3. Feed the ingredients one at a time, in the order listed, through the juicer.
4. Stir the juice and pour into glasses to serve.

PER SERVING

Calories: 99| Fat: 0.9g | Protein: 2.9g | Carbohydrates: 23.9g | Sugar: 16.9g

Orange and Ginger Root Energy Shot

Prep time: 5 minutes | Cook time: 0 minutes | Serves 1

½- to 1-inch piece fresh ginger root
1 small orange, peeled

1. Peel, cut, deseed, and/or chop the ingredients as needed.
2. Place a container under the juicer's spout.
3. Feed the ingredients one at a time, in the order listed, through the juicer.
4. Stir the juice and pour into glasses to serve.

PER SERVING

Calories: 100| Fat: 0.9g | Protein: 1.9g | Carbohydrates: 24.9g | Sugar: 0g

Strawberry and Romaine Juice with Carrots

Prep time: 5 minutes | Cook time: 0 minutes | Serves 2

1 large carrot
1 cup strawberries
8 medium romaine leaves
8 small celery stalks

1. Peel, cut, deseed, and/or chop the ingredients as needed.
2. Place a container under the juicer's spout.
3. Feed the ingredients one at a time, in the order listed, through the juicer.
4. Stir the juice and pour into glasses to serve.

PER SERVING

Calories: 101| Fat: 1.9g | Protein: 8.9g | Carbohydrates: 17.9g | Sugar: 5.9g

Gingery Cucumber and Kale Cilantro Juice

Prep time: 5 minutes | Cook time: 0 minutes | Serves 1

2 cups spinach
3 kale leaves
½ cucumber
1 green apple
2 tablespoons cilantro sprigs
½ lime
Fresh ginger root

1. Wash all the ingredients.
2. Trim the ends from the cucumber, then cut into 4-inch pieces.
3. Remove the apple core and discard. Cut the apple into quarters, leaving the peel intact.
4. Peel the lime and cut into quarters.
5. Slice off a ½-inch piece of the ginger root.
6. Place a pitcher under the juicer's spout to collect the juice.
7. Feed each ingredient through the juicer's intake tube in the order listed.
8. When the juice stops flowing, remove the pitcher and stir the juice.
9. Serve immediately.

PER SERVING

Calories: 102| Fat: 0.9g | Protein: 3.9g | Carbohydrates: 30.9g | Sugar: 15.9mg

Pear and Parsley with Orange Juice
Prep time: 5 minutes | Cook time: 0 minutes | Serves 2

1 medium navel orange
1 medium apple
1 medium pear
½ bunch parsley
½ lime

1. Peel, cut, deseed, and/or chop the ingredients as needed.
2. Place a container under the juicer's spout.
3. Feed the ingredients one at a time, in the order listed, through the juicer.
4. Stir the juice and pour into glasses to serve.

PER SERVING

Calories: 99| Fat: 0g | Protein: 0.9g | Carbohydrates: 26.9g | Sugar: 1.9mg

5 Minute Lime Kiwi and Orange Juice
Prep time: 5 minutes | Cook time: 0 minutes | Serves 2

3 medium navel oranges
3 ripe kiwis
1 teaspoon lime zest

1. Peel, cut, deseed, and/or chop the ingredients as needed.
2. Place a container under the juicer's spout.
3. Feed the oranges and kiwis through the juicer.
4. Stir the lime zest into the juice and pour into glasses to serve.

PER SERVING

Calories: 103| Fat: 0g | Protein: 1.9g | Carbohydrates: 26.9g | Sugar: 1.9mg

.

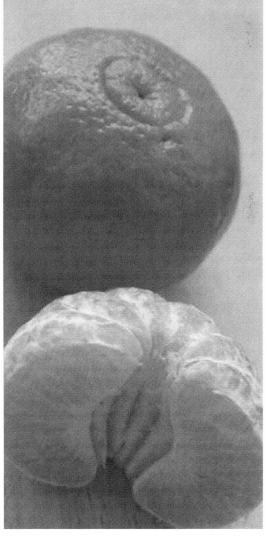

Appendix 1 Measurement Conversion Chart

Volume Equivalents (Dry)	
US STANDARD	**METRIC (APPROXIMATE)**
1/8 teaspoon	0.5 mL
1/4 teaspoon	1 mL
1/2 teaspoon	2 mL
3/4 teaspoon	4 mL
1 teaspoon	5 mL
1 tablespoon	15 mL
1/4 cup	59 mL
1/2 cup	118 mL
3/4 cup	177 mL
1 cup	235 mL
2 cups	475 mL
3 cups	700 mL
4 cups	1 L

Volume Equivalents (Liquid)		
US STANDARD	**US STANDARD (OUNCES)**	**METRIC (APPROXIMATE)**
2 tablespoons	1 fl.oz.	30 mL
1/4 cup	2 fl.oz.	60 mL
1/2 cup	4 fl.oz.	120 mL
1 cup	8 fl.oz.	240 mL
1 1/2 cup	12 fl.oz.	355 mL
2 cups or 1 pint	16 fl.oz.	475 mL
4 cups or 1 quart	32 fl.oz.	1 L
1 gallon	128 fl.oz.	4 L

Temperatures Equivalents	
FAHRENHEIT(F)	**CELSIUS(C) APPROXIMATE)**
225 °F	107 °C
250 °F	120 ° °C
275 °F	135 °C
300 °F	150 °C
325 °F	160 °C
350 °F	180 °C
375 °F	190 °C
400 °F	205 °C
425 °F	220 °C
450 °F	235 °C
475 °F	245 °C
500 °F	260 °C

Weight Equivalents	
US STANDARD	**METRIC (APPROXIMATE)**
1 ounce	28 g
2 ounces	57 g
5 ounces	142 g
10 ounces	284 g
15 ounces	425 g
16 ounces (1 pound)	455 g
1.5 pounds	680 g
2 pounds	907 g

Appendix 2 Index

MYRA J. BATTY

Made in the USA
Middletown, DE
02 May 2022